ATATÜRK
AND
TURKISM
TURKISH IDEALISM

Dr. Ali Nazmi Çora

1

Dr Dr. Ali Nazmi Çora

Dr. Ali Nazmi Cora is researcher, academician and author of over eighty books and many articles.
He has Received his Doctoral degree from Marmara University in Istanbul
He taught History and Political Science.
Dr Cora currenntly lives in South Florida, USA.

His Books

Research Books in English;

"Atatürk Faunder Father of the Modern Turkey", 2019, Atayurt Yayınevi
"Atatürk The lider of the Century and Atatürk's Thought System" 2019, KDP Amazon.com
"Turkısm. Turkish Idealism And Atatürk" 2019, KDP Amazon.com
"Economic Growth And Poverty Reduction", 2018, KDPAmazon.com
"Hydrogen Fuel of the Future", 2017, KDP Amazon.com

"Globalization and Regional Economic Integration", 2017, KDP Amazon.com
"Global Governance and Globalization", 2016, KDP Amazon.com
"The Global Economic Crises" 2016, KDP Amazon.com
"Armenian Genocide a Big Lie", 2015, KDP Amazon.com
"ISIS The Most Dangerous terrorist group" 2015, KDP Amazon.com
"Grand Turkey", 2013, KDP Amazon.com
"Development Among Turkey, NATO. European Union (EU) and European Security", 2013, KDP Amazon.com
"Patton vs Rommel", 2013, KDP Amazon.com

Research Books in Turkish:

"Atatürk Türk Ülküsü Türkçülük", (2019), Atayurt, Ankara
"Atatürk, Atatürkçü Düşünce Sistemi", (2019), Atayurt, Ankara
"28 Şubat Davası" 2018, KDP Amazon com
"Atatürk, Türk Tarihi ve MU uygarlığı" 2018, KDP Amazon com
"Dağlık Karabağ Sorunu" 2018, KDP Amazon com
"Türkiye'nin Stratejik Önemi" 2019, KDP Amazon com
"Terör, Trörizm ve Ayrılıkçı Kürt Sorunu" 2018, KDP Amazon com
"Ermeni Mezalimi ve Ömer Necati Gören tarafından anlatılanlar", 2015, KDP Amazon com
"Kürtler Türk'müdür?, 2015, KDP Amazon com
"Ayrılıkçı Kürt Sorunu", 2015, KDP Amazon com
TAVİSTOCK, Dünyayı Yöneten Örgüt", KDP 2015, Amazon com
"ÖRTÜLÜ SAVAŞ", 2015, Amazon com
"Sessiz Savaş ABD ve AVRUPA Sivil Toplum Örgütlerini (NGO) Kullanarak Bağımsız Ülkeleri Nasıl Yönetiyor", 2015, KDP Amazon com
"Evrende Yaşam" 2015, KDP Amazon com
"Uzay ve zaman" 2015, KDP Amazon com
"UFO ve Zaman Yolculuğu Teknolojisi-Time Travel Technology", 2015, KDP Amazon com
"Geleceğin Dünyası", 2014, KDP Amazon com
"Türk Birleşik Devletleri, Türk Birliği", 2014, KDP Amazon com
"Türkçülüğün Esasları", 2014, KDP Amazon com
"Tarih Türklerle Başlar", 2014, KDP Amazon com

"Atatürkçü Düşünce Sistemi, Uygarlık İdeolojisi", 2014, KDP Amazon com

"Atatürk ve Din, ", 2014, KDP Amazon com

"AGARTA", 2014, KDP Amazon com

"İnsandan Evrene", 2014, KDP Amazon.com

"Çekiç Güç, Tarihimizdeki Kara Leke", 2014, KDP Amazon com

"Atatürk'ün Fikir ve Düşünceleri", 2013, KDP Amazon com

"Çekiç Güç, Operation Provide Comfort,Huzur harekatı, Düzeltilmiş ikinci baskı", 2013, KDP Amazon com

"Ne Çektinbe Abi Şu E maillerinden-5", 2013, KDP Amazon com

"Ne Çektinbe Abi Şu E maillerinden-4", 2013, KDP Amazon com

"Ne Çektinbe Abi Şu E maillerinden-3", 2013, KDP Amazon com

"Ne Çektinbe Abi Şu E maillerinden-2", 2013, KDP Amazon com

"Ne Çektinbe Abi Şu E maillerinden-1", 2013, KDP Amazon com

"Azınlık Faaliyetleri", 2013, KDP Amazon com

"Türkiye'nin Stratejik Önemi", 2013, KDP Amazon com

"ABD'nin Milli Menfaatleri, Stratejisi ve Kuvvet yapısı", 2013, KDP Amazon com

"Nağme-I İştiyak", 2013, KDP Amazon com

"Türkiye, NATO, Avrupa Birliği (AB), Avrupa Güvenlik ve Savunma Politikasındaki (AGSP) Gelişmeler" (Tez), 2013, KDP Amazon com

"İstiklal harbi Sırasında Atatürk'ün Nutkuna ve Diğer Resmi Belgelere Göre Azınlıkların Faaliyetleri, Bunlara Karşı alınan Tedbirler", 2013, KDP Amazon com

"Yalan Ermeni Soykırımı İddiası", 2013, KDP Amazon com

"Yalan Ermeni Soykırımı İddiasının Bugünkü Durumu", 2013, KDP Amazon com

"Sözde Ermeni Soykırımı İddiası", 2013, KDP Amazon com

"Sözde Ermeni Soykırımı İddiasının Bugünkü Durumu", 2013, KDP Amazon com

"İçimizdeki şeytanlar", 2008, Toplumsal Dönüşüm

"Uluslararası terorizm ve failleri", 2008, Toplumsal Dönüşüm

"Çekiç Güç'ün Kürdistan Tuzağı", 2008, Toplumsal Dönüşüm

"Çekiç Güç'ün Gizli Günlüğü", 2008, Toplumsal Dönüşüm

"Tarihimizde Kara Leke Çekiç Güç", 2008, Toplumsal Dönüşüm

"Türk Komutanın İzlenimleri ile Çekiç Güç", 2008, Toplumsal Dönüşüm

"İrtica ve Terör", 2008, Toplumsal Dönüşümı

"Kürt Sorununun Geleceği", 2004, Q Matris
"Birleşik Türk Devletleri", 2004, Q Matris
"Türkiyenin geleceği", 2004, Q Matris
"Cybervision-Büyük Türkiye", 2000, İrfan

Enlightenment knowledge

In English;
"Esoterica", 2014, KDP Amazon.com
"Re-Youth", 2014, KDP Amazon.com
"Rejuvenate" 2013, KDP Amazon.com

In Turkish;
"İnsanları Anlamak", Kadim Seri No:3, 2017, KDP Amazon.com
"Yaşamından Zevk al", Kadim Seri No:2, 2017, KDP Amazon.com
"Düşüncenin Gücü", Kadim Seri No:1, 2017, KDP Amazon.com
"Bedenini sev", 2015, KDP Amazon.com
"Mutlu Bir hayat İçin", 2013, KDP Amazon com
"Düşüncenin Gücü", 2013, KDP Amazon com
"Hayat basittir", 2013, KDP Amazon com
"Yeniden Gençlik", 2013, Amazon com

Poetry Books;

"Ben Seni Sevdim", 2018, KDP Amazon.com
"Aşkıma Şiirler",2015, KDP Amazon.com

The study books for Turkish Command and Staff College ;

"Grup Çalışma tekniği" 1986, Harp Akademileri yayınları
"Yönetim" 1986, Harp Akademileri yayınları
"Askeri Mesele Çözme Teknikleri, Durum Muhakemesi, karargah Etüdü "
1986, Harp Akademileri yayınları
"Karargah Etüdü" 1986, Harp Akademileri yayınları
"İkinci Dünya Harbinin Unutulmayan İsimleri Patton ve Rommel" 1984,
Harp Akademileri yayınları

Dedication;

I would like to thank my wife for standing beside me throughout my career and writing this book. She has been my inspiration and motivation for continuing to improve my knowledge and move my career forward. I dedicate this book to my true love, my wife Nedret Çora for everything.

Dr. Ali Nazmi Çora

CONTENTS

"For his nation had been injustice and inharmonious; for it had been fraudulent and deceitful; for it had to set persous by the ears between the brothers; for it had backbited the ruler against his nation; Turkish nation had lost its province that it had made province and had lost its Khan that it had led to become Khan."

Kültigin Inscription Eastern Front,Lines 4-8 Mogolistan, (Gokturk State-SkyTurks (AD 7th century)

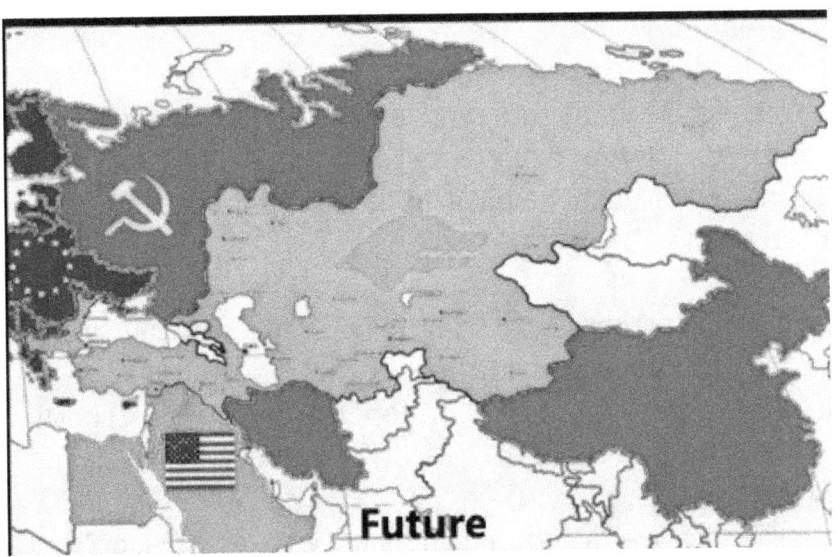

Since the Turkish nation had appeared in the historical stage as a political entity, many Turkic states have been established. These are political parts of a whole following each other similar to rings of a chain and also extensions of Turkish culture through out the time. All through the history Turkic states have expanded in a wide period of time and geographical scale. Among these states, there has been ones which have stayed in the stage of history for a very long time and presented political and cultural superiorities as well as ones those which had disintegrated in a very short period of time.

Existing, living and surviving your life freely and efficiently requires, and comprises precedence of POWER, in a certain period of TIME, and a certain PLACE. If the life in question is life of a nation, "place" then would mean life space-homeland and the country would mean the state. Undoubtedly, the dominating power; would become national power, state power. Time is history, it is process of independence, it is duration of nation's survival, and life schedule.

There are many nations on the earth, 185 different flags of different nations wave in front the United Nations building. Most of these nations are not yet even a quarter century old.

It is only Turkish nation which has up until today been able to protect her authentic national identity and uninterruptedly continue independent state structure since the centuries before Christ, Turkish state is eternal.

Turks have always claimed their national values, cultures and tradition. Putting previous Turkic states aside, it has been 700 years only since the beginning of Ottoman Empire. Consider that, Ottoman State had been 192 years old when the American continent was discovered. It is obvious that Turkey has very prosperous and deep state experience.

To realize this fact it is enough to have a look at a world history atlas each page of which is designed to demonstrate the change in political boundaries in every half centuries as well as culture and civilization centers of 27 centuries. In this 27 centuries of time there had emerged very few numbers of states with an outstanding, global character and could become a super power.

Turkish nation in the old world had been a central super power of the world, and also a unique state that could continentally attain this super big state position for a very long time.

22 million square miles of a land comprised of three continents, suitable for settlement, had for hundred of years been ruled by various Turkic societies, governments and states. Moreover, this land had always preserved the characteristic of being the homeland for continuous Turkish presence, culture and language on the long axis of Eurasian continental block.

Saka, Khoan, Western Khoan, Avar, Hazar, Gokturk, Grand Selcuklu, Kuman, Pecenek, Kipcak, Harzemli, Anatolian Selcuklu, Cengizli, Çagatayli, Ilhanli, Altin ordulu, Timurlu, Akkoyunlu, Karakoyunlu, Safevi, Baburlu, Ottaman life and sovereignty areas should be remembered.

16th century is named as Turkish Century. Following this year Turkistism reached all around 15 million square miles in three different continents and under the roof of four different states. It should always be remembered that the area of Ottoman Empire which had constituted the Western side of Turkistism had exceeded 15 million square miles

At his historical speech at the 10th anniversary of the Turkish Republic, Atatürk said: "Today Soviet Republic is our friend and ally. We are in need of this friendship. However, no one can today asses what is going to happen to himself tomorrow. Just like the Ottomans, or Austria-Hungary, anyone can disintegrate any time. The world can reach a new balance. At that point Turkey should know what she is going to do...We have brothers of same religion, same believing and same essence living under the authority of this friend of ours.

Being prepared does not simply mean silently waiting for that day to come. It is necessary to get prepared. How could nations get prepared to this? The answer is; by keeping their moral bridges resistant enough. Language is a bridge...Believing is a bridge...History is a bridge..."

"...We should go deep down our roots and get integrated in our history which had been separated by events. We should wait for their (Exterior Turk's) approaching to us. We should also approach to them..." he said.

Apparently, series of significant occasions occurring in the world in the last years, shows that forty hundred years old political balances are now facing the change.

In fact, the uneasiness and challenges we are facing today arise from overwhelmed old balances and that new balances have not been well constructed in their place.

CHAPTER-ONE

TURKISM
TURKISH IDEALISM

"IDEAL" whose lexical meaning is "OATH", "REMOTE TARGET" and "CONSUMMATION" is such a force that moves the community in the same path that people seem to have inwardly promised each other for this cause.

Ideal is first born in the hearts of people, in the depths of the hearts, in their subconscious minds, in their dreams and manifests itself first in the epics. Then it passes to conscious mind, is explained by National Leaders. Then big heroes make big moves to fulfil it. They run after these moves voluntarily. In the midst of all these struggles the nation walks and advances first spiritually then physically, grows mature and thrives.

National ideals are energy sources that will keep the nations alive for centuries.

Idealistic nations are full of self-sacrificing people. The abundance of self-sacrificing people means the dominance of all sorts of human virtues. Human societies live with human virtues. Societies that have lost their humanity are doomed to collapse, even if they are in prosperity and seem to be great from an external view. Like the ancient Roman Empire.

However, those which have capacity and energy run after the greatness ideal. Because the greatness ideal is actually the ideal of great sacrifices. That's why cowards and inferiors are afraid of greatness, always wanting to remain small.

Turkism is the name of Turkish Nationalism. If one asks what the Turkism is, who the Turk is,

It can be explained as "those who feel themselves Turks, can sacrifice themselves for Turkey, Turkish ness and Turkish Union, do beneficial things for Turkey, Turkism and Turkish Unity and endeavour for this purpose, who can shout with his whole existence "how happy am I to say I am Turk" wherever they live, be it Turkey or Antarctica".

The suffix at the end of the word Turkism might indicate membership, love or advocacy depending on the context. Since Turkism is also Turkish love and advocacy, the word is used correctly. Turkish advocacy or Turkish love of other nations cannot be expressed with this word. As a matter of fact, that other nations love Turks does not indicate a real love but a temporary kindness, interest, political necessities.

Nobody loves Turks except for Turks.

Turkism is an ideal. Ideals are moral nourishment for nations. Even the most fortunate one of the nations without ideals is doomed to remain faint. If such nations are not fortunate, it is inevitable that they will be defeated, overwhelmed and even disappear.

Turkism is the ideal of all Turks uniting to be a single state and being advanced and superior to all nations in every way.

It is the name of our national ideal. This name can be summarized by "Turkish Unity". Ideals are great wishes which are born as a blend of reality and dream, look for tomorrow looking at yesterday, accelerate nations and for which people sacrifice. Nations have the right to live as much as they can die.

Turkism is the unconditional sovereignty and independence of Turks in Turkish country and the advancement and superiority of Turkishness in every way in comparison with all the other nations.

Turkism is the ideal of all Turks uniting to be a single state and being advanced and superior to all nations in every way.

Turkism is in favor of Turkization of Turks in every respect. There will be nothing foreign within these borders. Turkish culture will prevail unconditionally. In this respect, Turkism has its own language, history and alphabet notion.

Turkism is a belief as well as an idea. Because it is a belief, it is undisputedly accepted without criticism. Disputable part open to criticism is not its core but its details.

Turkism does not serve to rise, but to raise. Enhancement of communities depends on the majority of altruistic individuals.

The purpose of our ideal is to move Turkish nation to the front line of contemporary civilization as the crow flies, without begging others, jumping over the eras and to make the nation the strongest in the world in science, technique, civilisation, human rights and equality, environmentalism and to uplift Turkishness.

Our case as the Turkists is to glorify the presence of the Turkish nation and to sustain it forever. There is no other idea and no other case above this one. Any act that does not serve the idea of preserving the existence of the Turkish nation, raising it and maintaining it forever, will not be valid for the Turkish nation.

The Turkish nation has its own realities, conditions, history, national traditions and a national spirit. The Turkish nation cannot develop and survive by copying the systems created according to the conditions of the foreign countries. This idea can only be possible with a hundred percent national system which takes national realities of Turkish nation, national spirit into account and which follows modern science and modern technique,is respectful and adheres to Turkish history and national traditions, national morals, religion.

Written by Has Hacib Yusuf in 11th century, "Kutadgu Bilig" means "knowledge of politics". "Kut" which means "fortune, bliss" has been mistranslated as "knowledge which gives happiness" so far. The meaning of this name, as implied by the content of the great piece, is political treatise. Because it puts forward the necessary conditions for the society to be happy, it is revealed that

Turks' understanding of politics depends on "the science of social happiness". In fact in the famous Orkhon Inscriptions which was erected by Bilge Kagan for his hero brother Kül Tegin three centuries before Kutadgu Bilig and by Icen Kagan for his father, they wrote that they succeeded in gaining victories, feeding the nation, providing their clothing and increase in their population, i.e. they succeeded in making them happy.

At the present time, the principle of thinking only today and escaping dangers, instead of maintaining a political attitude to make the nation happy has become widespread. Despite Ataturk's carefully considered and if necessary dashing policy, Ismet Inonu only tried to govern the state with a policy that is well thought out, but so prudent that it made him fall into errors.

A nation might be spared from dangers for a long time with a policy that is too prudent. Nevertheless, because too prudent policies are passive administrations, they can never eloign enemy states and when it falls due they can never prevent them from attacking.

For this reason there is no national benefit in conducting a policy of getting on well with everyone instead of national policy. Nations are reputable and powerful based on their national demands. Furthermore, "national demands" in other word "ideals" are nations' source of courage, dynamic power and unity motive.

Since Ataturk's death Turkey has been conducting a passive state policy. Turkey intensified this passive policy on the basis of this foundation, seeming to adopt the words "Peace at home, peace in the world," as the place and era necessitates just for that era; unfortunately a mentality of not offending anyone for the sake of peace has prevailed, and this mentality has caused the neglect of Turks outside political borders. The thought that attending to Turks living in any country will offend, disturb and annoy that particular country, led world Turkism to be virtually denied.

However, the view of the world is noteworthy in this respect. No nation, including the black people of Africa ever stops attending to their fellow race. Especially that tiny Greece tries to pull Epirus apart from Albania while at the same time yearning for Cyprus and carrying out ruses to resurrect Byzantium in the time to come.

There has been constant struggle and competition among nations since the earliest times in history. Every nation makes relentless effort to raise its existence and to dominate over other societies. To be unaware of this struggle between nations is to ignore the rigid truths of life and to pretend not to know them. In our era, in which it is claimed that civilization and technique have gone far forward, the struggle for superiority, power and welfare among nations continues in full blast. "Right belongs to power" principle has been the only one to be valid when it comes to relations between nations, since the dawn of the time.

Yet, we Turks have ruled with right and justice throughout history. But the indispensable condition of making the right dominate is to be strong. It should not be forgotten that the propaganda of protecting the world peace and respecting the rights of the nations, no matter how well-intentioned, cannot disrupt the principle of "Rights belongs to power".

Making war is necessary to live. Because people have not found a remedy other than war when it comes to ending cases with conflict of national interests. There are two means that make people stand ready for war. One is material; we call it "technique". The other is moral; we call it "ideal". Throughout history, it has been seen that the one who is morally superior wins the collision between the equal material forces. Moral force can create technical force. Lack of moral power means defeat, no matter how great the material power is.

What is Moral Force?

The Turkish ideal is the desire and belief of Turkish greatness and Turkish force. Faith is the greatest moral creator. With faith, even hopeless patients recover. National supremacy faith is the desire to grow, that is, national ideal. National ideals are the creative forces of communities. Like all creative powers, it also has the property of destroying separations and disagreements.

The Turkish creative power or the Turkish ideal, is a thought which has been a principle for several centuries, for which people have fought, which has been realized a few times. Those who call it a dream are the ones who have become loose and lazy. Would it be realized if it were a dream as they say?

Other than that, 20th century became a time of miracles and what was thought to be impossible was made possible. In this respect, it is a right for people to hope for the realization of the Turkish ideal. Today's ideals are completely national. The national ideal, which also includes religious beliefs, is this feeling and thought that drive, empower and ennoble people.

In today's vulgar materialism, the Turkish ideal seems to have turned yellow and to have incinerated a bit.

When materialism sickness subsides it will shine again. Therefore, we are obliged to embrace the Turkish ideal. Our only weapon against the ingrained hostility and grudge of the West which defeated all the East nations except for Turks, is the Turkish ideal.

It is not always adventurous to think about the expat citizens, to want them to merge with us or at least to be independent. All the nations of the world, even the new state founders, primarily consider their expat fellow people. Being a great nation with its past and today, we have to consider our expat citizens and especially after the bill of rights, we have to make attempts for them to enjoy human rights.

On the basis of the United Nations constitution, which we have signed, it is both our national debt and humanitarian duty to support the independence of Turks outside of our political boundaries and to help them rid themselves of foreign domination. While the societies that have not even gotten over the cannibalism era are given the right to establish a state, we cannot accept that the Turks, who are civilized and highly capable, pursue their lives as prisoners here and there.

We are confident that a well-functioning and sensible, principled Turkish foreign affairs in faithful hands will introduce this right to the whole world. In national ideals, there are three periods from less to more: Independence, unity, conquests.

1. The first period of national ideal is to win independence. Those who are not independent go for winning it, those who have won independence, on the other hand, go for the thought of protecting and strengthening it.

2. The second period of national ideal is unity. In other words bringing all individuals of a nation under a single flag, a single state. The first task of every nation that has gained independence is to seek ways to save those who have been strangled by foreign stripes. Or, if a nation lives an independent life in several separate states, it also engages in political and military efforts to unite them.

3.- The third period of the national ideal is the conquest. Today conquests are made through capital, through culture.

Wouldn't it be an advocate ideal? Can't a nation conduct the ideal to live in abundance and reach happiness within the borders it owns?

No! Because the idea of protecting the boundaries and being rich can never be an ideal. These are the smallest and most common wishes for a nation. An ideal is not a small and usual request. Ideal, mixed with a little imagination, is a distant and difficult goal. Ideal is a blissful and sweet thought that lets the members of a nation burning with desire for that ideal live in excitement. Ideals feed on blood, sacrifice and heroism.

A nation sheds blood like rivers, makes supreme sacrifices in order to reach its ideal. Ideals are reached through blood, sword, combat and grudge. Ideals require brave hearts, haymaker, unshakable will, high morals. Ideal is a religion. It requires heroes and martyrs.

Those who deny ideals and conduct humanitarian efforts (!) not to discomfort themselves can be encountered anytime, anywhere. But after a large majority in a nation believes in the national ideal, the remaining ones must necessarily obey this national movement.

What is important to us is to prevent frenemy foreigners' sabotaging the national ideal as though for the sake of national interest.

If you put common ideal aside in a society you see that people lose their humanity. In a community where we find no common thought, everyone only thinks of their own interest and pleasure. There is no sacrifice, respect, courtesy in such a community. Selfishness, vulgarity, bribery, favouritism and all sorts of dishonesty are rampant.

Will a materialistic person die for the country? Will a selfish person help the needy persons? Doesn't a man who doesn't believe in his nation cooperate with the foreigner? Someone who considers virtue ridiculous doesn't steal and whisk?

The characteristics of embarrassment, involvement in an ideal and being able to die for creed and an idea are what distinguish human from animal. Abashed people avoid committing crime and being accused. A person who is devoted to the ideal puts up with financial problems without complaining. One who dies in the name of a creed and idea plays an extraordinary role in the edification of those who are his successors. They have nothing to do with matter.

Only considering individuals' welfare while contemplating the development of Turkey does not suffice to strengthen the country. A country which lives in prosperity and is advanced is doomed to be demolished unless it is superior in terms of morals and idea. Because nations without individuals to die for an idea will escape from death in case of an enemy attack, their welfare will not make any difference.

However, as Turks, for centuries, have had the ideal of establishing a great country, developing them is easier than developing other countries in the same circumstances. Turkish nation has the ability to make the development move based on sacrifice faster than many other nations. Yet, Turkish society, having been ruled by mighty leaders for centuries, requests great guides as it has been the case in every era of its history.

The biggest benefit of great leaders with national consciousness and pride is to protect the society from having inferiority complex. To be able to do great things, a nation must believe that it is a great nation. Although Turkish nation was far behind today's conditions in terms of population, fortune, technique and culture in Atatürk's era, it was so powerful in terms of moral strength and that's why the nation found in it the faith and strength to overcome all sorts of dangers.

But if leaders and intellectuals have inferiority complex it is impossible for that nation to develop. Because the illusion saying that development moves are futile is engraved in the soul and hearts are filled with despair. Victory can never be won by those who think they are destroyed.

The development move will undoubtedly be through science methods. But if our society's social and individual psychology, history, national traditions, social structure are not considered, scientific methods will not provide success. Because, just as the same medication does not have the same effect on individuals with the same illness, scientific methods do not have the same effect on every society.

The science method also orders to be freed from pre-

thoughts. For this reason, it is time for the Turkish nation to speak openly about what its political regime should be. Regimes are not targets, they are only means for the sake of nation's happiness. Therefore nations, throughout their history have sometimes changed regimes. In a sense, regime is the dress of the nations. Nations also, like individuals, wear clothes in accordance with time and place. As a flaxen dress whose neck is open, which is for warm places would cause a person die in cold climate regions, this or that regime might sometimes prepare a nation's demolition.

Today, according to the political and social conditions that we are in, the most suitable dress for us, in other words the most suitable regime is democracy. This idea has settled in our nation day by day and this is also the regime of our allies that we have to move together.

However, our determination to remain in a democratic regime can never prevent us from respecting our non-democratic history and our heroes filling us with pride. Because a nation that despises its past, can only be a community full of dishonest people. We must also keep out of sight that the success of democracy is directly proportional to the strength of the national consciousness in society.

Speaking of development of the Turkish nation, it must be the principal condition that the development target is Great Turkey in order to assign this movement a meaning that would fill the hearts with excitement and would lead citizens to sacrifice and heroism. Superior and advanced Turkey with its culture, science, technique as well as its morals and virtues. Otherwise, a move for only welfare and prosperity is not any different from company moves

Companies and states are different things. And the communities that confuse being a state with being a commercial institution are always doomed to live in the shadow of others and to collapse in the first impact.

One of the conditions of being a great state is to have a rich and mighty language. Making our language, which is strong in terms of its roots but which is not developed due to national neglects, a great language for science and art is a crucial case of ours which cannot be neglected. Neither hybrid old language nor factoid pure Turkish can be a great language of art and science. Terminology derivation based on Turkish roots, picking Turkish option or what is made Turkish in speaking language are based on 'purified Turkish' notion. Language for a nation equals his/her heart for a person. This valuable asset must be protected by experts with national consciousness, media, artists and an academy which will be established in accordance with real values.

Societies that want to live as nation, jealously protect their national characteristics. That the Scots wear skirts or the Indian clothes that are weird for us?

As another characteristic of becoming a high nation, to enact strong laws and to make respect a belief, all sorts of precautions must be taken and instead of translation of other codes, laws should be enacted depending on national tradition and contemporary law principles. Laws must be the ones that protect the state, nation, national culture, morality, order, family, individuals, honor and rights; the justice measure should be provided with the most precise balance.

Since the state is, in theory, an institution established to protect the lives of citizens and ensure their happiness, the socialist understanding of insuring every Turkish person against disease and unemployment is the most fundamental factor to ensure peace of mind.

The morality of a nation, especially of youth, is important. Because when it comes to the destiny of a nation, youth will shed blood and function. If youth is provided with examples of morality or moral discipline in the surrounding environment, they think immorality will always be overwhelmed, but if the same youth witnesses that bribery, favoritism, flattery and injustice prevail in contrast with moral prompting, then a moral crisis rises.

Turkish morality has been socialist since the oldest ages. In other words, the interest of the society in Turks is valued above those of people. Along with this, powerful persons have been beneficial for the society and they have always been paid respect. Turkish morality, which does not value individuality, respects personality.

The job is until we enter the sea. After entering the cold goes away. You also start to make great strokes peculiar to good swimmers with great skill.

We are friends of nations, ideas and people that do not harm us. However, we believe that it is a great misconception to think that life works with love alone. Everything in the world exists with its opposite. Therefore, along with love there is also grudge. Turkism is, in a sense, "hostility to hostility against Turkishness".

Welfare and fortune alone do not bring a society happiness. They only bring a brutish comfort. Because happiness is every state felt with spiritual pleasures and it is peculiar to people. Moral values which we call as spirit exist only in humans.

In order for our nation to live and thrive, it is necessary, above everything, to beat as a united heart, to exist as a united soul, to be a united voice, in unity and solidarity. Today, although we have suffered many catastrophes, one of the greatest nations of the world is the Turkish nation.

From the Danube river, from the Balkan mountains to China, there are still Turks and people still pass through Turkish lands. The great things this great nation did in history and its great existence in the worry certain foreign forces and foreign circles who have eye on this region and who worry about the strengthening of Turkish nation. For this purpose, in order for the development of the Turkish nation, every Turk should always consider principally, to preserve the unity, to stand against every organisation that would take us to pieces, alienate us from each other, make us enemies. Regionalism is one of the primary threats for our unity. Another one is sectarianism.

In order for Turkish nation to develop, it should, above all, return to its national identity and to its national essence. Rising of a nation could only be possible with creating national assets. A nation could only protect its power and rise as owner of morals, by laying claim to its religion, creed, morality, traditions, history and conventions. A nation which becomes distant from its self, despises its own identity, does not like itself, thinks others superior to itself, considers copying others as merit loses itself and is already dead. That's why we emphasize in our struggle for the development of our nation, above all, that: We are Turkish, we are similar to ourselves, we are a strong, skilled, virtuous, moral nation.We have no deficiencies compared to other nations

It is not possible to rise by copying others. We will rely on our own self, we will rely on ourselves, we will return to our own characteristics. But we will also take the modern science and modern technique and find the remedies for development of the country as soon as possible.

Nevertheless, freedom in Turkey should be precisely defined for activities that will be useful to the Turkish nation. There cannot be no freedom for acts that will harm the Turkish nation, ruin it and pose a danger to its life. Freedom to destroy the Turkish nation, freedom to demolish the Turkish nation cannot be recognized in this land.

The Turkish nation has many national characteristics, traditions and beliefs, which make it invincible and which make it overcome every catastrophe to date, disrupt every danger throughout its thousands of years of history. The main one of these is its character not accepting defeat and its idea to protest indulgence. The refusal to surrender, the refusal to be defeated, is the secret of invincibility. No matter how dark the situation is, no matter how improbable our circumstances are, never accepting defeat and never accepting to surrender are the eternal Turkish slogans. The Turkist is a fearless human who holds the national interests above individuals, respects the national sacred values and the past, has a high morality of duty, and has no fear when it comes to fighting.

A Turkist cannot be a gallivanter or a sycophantic person. He likes to live hard and shows the greatest toughness against the desires of his flesh. He has to be modest, respects his national heroes, but he doesn't hesitate to tell if national heroes have errors, and he never dignify someone, who is not hero, with heroism title. In particular, he never forgives those who demolish sacred values of Turkishness and considers those who forgive them as enemies. While doing a service to his nation, he does this because he considers the service as task and he knows that even the biggest service he can do will be very small compared to the service of the martyrs who died without being known.

Turkism favours "disciplined nation". "Disciplined people" means that people have accepted the system of mutual rights and duties asserting that individuals will not harm the state and the state will not harm the individuals.

At the beginning of every move Turks make is to rise working in one's area of expertise. Every Turkist must work seriously and systematically to attain the highest rank of his profession.

If every Turkist makes his duty with faith, the ideal of Turkism becomes stronger and Turkishness becomes solid.

The first task of the Turkist people is to do their tasks with a pure mind and faithful heart.

Turks will be strengthened with Turkism, they will survive, they will advance and they will rise.

If a nation cannot carry the will to rise, does not trust itself, if it cannot do anything other than imitation, does not boast the past, does not want to be superior to others, does not face up to death for the ideal, if it is afraid of war, then that nation is rotten within.

To be able to survive today it is not enough be to as strong as before. Because you need to be stronger, too tough, too hard, too brave. The secret of this is to stick to the Turkism ideal. History does not forgive the nations which are deviated, coward, confused.

The ideal of Turkism demands from us pitiless morality of duty. If a soldier does his training tirelessly, if a teacher does his teaching job without weariness, if an officer continues to ease the public without getting angry, if a student tries to learn the lesson and if all tasks and the harmony between the ranks are established without flattery, indifference, show, if those below do not consider the order of a superior as priggery and if a superior does not get angry with rightful warnings of those below, if there are no such things as kindness at the level of hypocrisy and toughness at the level of rudeness in all mutual contacts, the duty will be fulfilled.

There are historical enemies of nations that have relied on an ideal and have committed themselves to it. These nations may have made friendship agreements with the enemy nation. These temporary friendships have no value. Historical enemies are only friends of foreign secretaries. Never a friend for the nation!

One of the biggest dangers for a nation is to sleep by swallowing peace and friendship opium. A nation which does not want to grow is doomed to shrink. A nation, which does not attack, is attacked.

Those who are in the responsible positions of the states may utter some words due to political courtesy or interest. But those who speak to the youth of the nation, i.e. teachers, poets, journalists, writers, and media workers who shape the society, should strengthen and support Turkism at every opportunity, everywhere.

Turkish Custom: First of all to love the Turkish nation and to believe in the power, the greatness of the Turkish nation.

Turkish Custom means high sense of duty. The Turkish Custom is based on the service of the nation and respect for the people in state service, and also in human relations. Turkish custom means respect for elders, affection and love for little ones.

The Turkish nation is loyal, solemn, serious, speaks shortly but to the point when necessary, does not get angry suddenly, it is cold-blooded, brave, ethical, determined, faithful to the word and duty.

In Europe, to refer to an honest promise, "A Turkish Promise?" they ask. They know that Turkish word can be trusted. Not to leave the order of superior, to show affection, compassion to minor ones and to keep them under obedience, to abide by God are the main elements of Turkish tradition. Turks established all their states with this tradition. The power of the Turkish nation came from the Turkish Ceremony. The Turkish Nation has suffered a disaster because its tradition was shaken, destroyed, and broken. The promise made in the Turkish Tradition is important. A Turk makes no random commitments. He doesn't promise randomly. He is dignified. He is not sloppy. He has nerves like steel. There is no returning back for a Turk once a promise is made.

Another requirement of the Turkish Tradition is a high sense of duty. It is to do the duty at all costs. Another requirement is to make every kind of sacrifice for the sake of society. It is renunciation of personal interest and pleasures for the sake of service to society. It is to give up. People sacrifice themselves for the nation. Greatness of the Turkish nation takes shape in this manner. Turkey will live like this and will rise like this. You will keep her alive, you will make her rise. Another most important requirement of the Turkish Tradition is to keep secrets.

Another requirement of the Turkish Tradition is knowing one's place. Knowing one's place... You will not ride the high horse, despise others or you will not deprecate yourself, despise yourself.

Adopting a new life philosophy that acknowledges modern science depending on the sense of Turkishness and high morality as leader, to realise Turkism ideal, to awaken the Turkish nation, to give them new vitality and momentum, everyone should be guided to working hard and movement. It is to make the big move by informing our citizens of the internal and external dangers surrounding us and by attributing our country's salvation and rise struggle to our public. Another way of realising the ideal is to raise intellectuals that will lead the nation and to make them people who are full of public love and away from selfinterest, like the public, who live with the public and work for the public and thus to integrate intellectuals and the public.

As Turkists, we must move forward by getting over every obstacle and not being afraid of anything in order to provide the best, the most beautiful and the highest for the Turkish Nation. We don't have much time to waste if we want to reach our goal.

We are Turkist, we are the people who struggle to preser ve the existence of the Turkish nation and to keep them up to eternity. This is our main principle. This is the main law for a Turk and everyone who says "I am Turk". Every idea and every act should comply with and realize this.

It is enough to look at examples to understand what a great force is the ideal that gives national faith and power to nations.

The Jews are cases in point when it comes to having an ideal. Today, this nation is battling bravely for the sake of a national ideal. National heroes grow up and national heroes die by giving honor to their nation. With their national ideal, half a million Jews in Palestine are challenging the whole world, not only Arabs. Thanks to sticking to the national ideal, they become a nation that is influential in the world.

We, on the other hand, while seeming to have faith in the saying "A Turk is better than whole world", deny ourselves. We were afraid of greatness. We adopted smallness and made fun of the national ideal as madness.

Nations are captured by their moral and intellectual forces before they are destroyed by the armies and other material forces of foreign forces. Enslavement and disappearance of a society in such a situation become definite. The main principles that constitute the power source of nations and that enhance societies are as follows:

1- To have a high, strong moral belief and sound ethics.
2- To have a strong spirit of national consciousness and nationalism.
3- To reach the highest level in science and technique.
4- To be able to produce with modern and up to date technology in industry and agriculture.

Although they seem to be simple at first glance, these principles show the unique way to nations' power, welfare and happiness. The Turkish Nation has been involved in vulgar strifes which have nothing to do with real enhancement and which are related to apery and formalism for two centuries instead of giving thought to these main issues.

For Turkish intellectuals and Turkish rulers, the asylum of western countries was adopted as an ideal. When our armies began to be defeated by European armies, these intellectuals wanted to understand where the force of Europe came from and to take that force. "Let's study in Europe, let's take these cultures and ideas, let us return to the country" they said.

But those who went to Europe could not get these principles, they took the West's luxury life based on consumption and waste, so they thought and claimed that they would be civilized in this way. They looked at Europe; they used jackets, ties, looked at women; how they were dressed, what they drank; whiskey, champagne, how they enjoyed themselves; New Year's Eve, pines were cut, they put the trees in their houses and had fun around it until the morning. Thus they said if we do these, if we dress up like them, eat, drink and have fun like them we will be civilized and Europeanized, as well. This was what they did and they did not think about the solution to increase the production of the Turkish nation.

An intellectual class which has no connection with the public and rural people has come into existence stucked in Istanbul, Ankara, Izmir and a few other major cities. A class that mimics European luxury like a monkey! They despised a class of people who saw signs of civilization in themselves as "reactionist".

For 250 years, the Turkish Nation has sought to recreate the conditions of being a strong state, a prosperous society and country, and to regain its former glory. To this end, there have been two attitude struggles;

1- A group claimed that "if we return to Sunnah-i-Sharif based life again, we'll have the old majesty". This group which is called "Kadizadeliler" considered Sunnah-i Sharif as wearing loose robe instead of casual clothes, eating with hands and not using spoon, destroying domes and minarets of mosques, not touching teeth with things like toothpick.

2- The opposing group said, Europeanization is a cure-all and they put forward the necessity of wearing dress, fez and sitting on chair instead of couch.

The Eighteenth Century passed with the struggles of these two groups, riots, coups and revolutions. This continued until Interregnum (1807) and finally ended with "Sened-i Ittifak (Charter of Alliance)" with the final victory of those who were in favor of Europeanism.

In fact, the Kadızadeliler as much as the Europeanists, were in the pursuit of equally formal, soulless, coreless claims. If this group called üstüvaniler had won instead of Europeanists, the result would have been the same. We would be at about the same spot in the scale of underdeveloped countries whose intellectuals wear loose robe instead of pants.

It's been about 160 years on the way of Europeanism. Every fashion has been practiced in this period of time. They tried Admiral Mustafa Reşit English liberalism, Admiral Mithat French parliamentarism, Menderes American pragmatism.

The most radical property reforms, the sharpest reforms of the army were made. The Janissary army was bombarded and the timar holder organization was displaced. From Admiral Mithat Constitutionalism to Sultan Hamit authoritarianism, every experience was gone through but it could not be prevented that the borders shrank from Crimea to Aras, from Yemen to Antep and from Baghdad to Hakkari.

One party system, multi-party democracy, assembly, all have been implemented. Nowadays, young people and intellectuals are being dragged after another imitation. However, Turkey's rise cannot be realized with imported ideas. No foreigner can think of the interests of the Turkish Nation as much as the Turkish Nation itself.

Today, with the ideas of communism, fascism or capitalism imported from abroad, the Turkish nation is wanted to be destroyed. Young Turkish people should revolt against destructive movements of thought which come from outside and which are imported to ensure others' interests not those of Turks.

The solution can only be possible by returning to ourselves, collaborating as a solid unity and working day and night.

CHAPTER-TWO

IDEALISM

Ideal means, as a word **"OATH", "REMOTE TARGET" AND "PURPOSE"** . Idealism is a struggle for a supreme purpose for which no sacrifice will be avoided. Idealism looks like the Western words 'ideal, idealism, idealistic' but they are not the same. It has a stronger meaning.

Idealism or ideal means to achieve what is in the human mind, to achieve the most perfect, the most beautiful, to design goals that will make them happy and to put effort, to work for achieving these goals.

Without the idealists among human beings, humanity would not be able to provide many of the developments that enlightened the world, and the rise in many areas. ·

Every truth, every idea first arises as a dream in people's minds. People dream. They imagine. These dreams indicate what is good for them, what they long for, what they would be happy to achieve and some other passions.

Greatness of people is directly proportional with their dreams. Dreams distinguish humans from animals and by these dreams they attain human title. So idealism is designation of a dream and shaping it in human brain that would provide happiness for people or groups when achieved, provide an enhanced circumstance. There are idealists in every society, there are national idealists, and the existence of idealists and national idealists is a great fortune for societies.

What is the ideal we think for the Turkish nation?
First of all, that the Turkish nation is at the highest level in morality, spirituality (heart power and morale) and in human senses, it lives in these conditions and it is advanced in science and technique and it is economically developed, devised its agriculture depending on modern technique and established modern industry, that it is a country with welfare. These ones constitute the majority of the principles that are adopted by a Turkish idealist for the sake of Turkish nation.

There are other targets within the borders of Turkish nationalism and idealism. These targets are that the Turkish nation comes to a point where it begs no mercy from anyone, it can survive on its own, that it can protect its existence with its own power and dominate the world. Along with this, it is the thought wishing the Turkish nation to be able to make itself known to the world all the time, and in addition to this sparing Turks from enslavement and living under foreign mandate, all become independent in accordance with the principle of self determination supporting determining one's own fate. These are all principles of idealism.

Moreover, the idea wishing that the Turkish nationalists within our idealism belonging to various professional groups attain the most advanced, the highest, the most beneficial results for the sake of both own nation and humanity, will also be included. A Turkish nationalist will always take into account the idealism for his own nation, and he will conduct both his idealism and his works in an integrated situation with both idealism and his own area.

Ideals are far targets in the long run. It may not be possible for an ideal to come into existence immediately. Ideals might continue for years and centuries to come. But ideals are lights illuminating a person's heart. Ideal is a guide that allows people to determine their direction. For the nations, the national ideal is the nation's guide, is the sun that illuminates the way of the nation. Humans without ideal are like ships without compass.

For this, every Turkish nationalist will be an idealist, will surely be an ideal owner. He will both have national ideal and humanity ideal. He will both have ideals regarding his job in which he will be successful to develop as a beneficial person and will serve to his society and nation to carry on fruitful business.

The human family consists of the gathering of all members of the world, of separate members of the nations. If a person wants to be human, wants to serve humanity, he must first serve his own nation, try to raise his nation and make his nation happy. If he does this, he will be serving humanity at the same time. Because if a person thinks of his own family and remains loyal to it, human feelings will reach the most mature level and he will be beneficial and loyal to people outside of his family.

If a human cannot be useful to his own nation, if he is not faithful to his own nation, it is only a fantasy to think that he will take into account humanity. Man should ensure prosperity, goodness, happiness and honor of the land in which he was raised, the nation in which he was born. If he does this, he will be serving humanity as well, since he is a part of humanity.

Our idealism is to raise the Turkish nation to the highest level of modern civilization as soon as possible, to make it happy, prosperous, independent, free, to have a life with its own rights.

Freedom of people, **independence** are our primary principles. People are born with free and equal rights. Apart from their capabilities and duties, people must be fully granted their rights. People should be recruited and placed in a queue according to their personal successes and abilities. Along with this equality of opportunity should be provided to all without discrimination.

Is there anything belonging to the Turks who are outside our present borders that can be included in our idealism? Answer is Yes. Anyone who has a Turkish name is within the circle of our love and interest. We can't give up on this. This is a natural right of Turkish nation as it is a natural right for every nation. Today's United Nations Constitution declares the principle of self-determination to every nation living on earth as a sacred principle.

The self-determination right is defined as a sacred right even for black people who live in Africa and who have never been able to establish any independent state and it is the most natural and sacred right for all Turks to want that Turks living under foreign or colonial domination get rid of these and attain independence, to wish these, to have good intentions about these while black people spare themselves from foreign or colonial domination and attain independence.

However, we base our idealism on reality and try to be as realistic as possible and not to put Turkey at risk in operations we undertake. Our idealism is not an idea of adventure. Our idealism is one that wants the Turkish nation rise to the highest level of modern civilization as soon as possible, to attain a prosper and happy life, to reach to a spot where it can survive on its own and to live independently and with sovereignty away from all sorts of fear and force.

This ideal also includes showing interest and love to all Turks, wishing their happiness and trying to ensure their happiness without putting Turkey at risk or exposing Turkey to dangers.

Idealism is a difficult occupation. Every man cannot be expected to achieve it. Because it is sacrificing your life not for success that can be attained in short period of time but for a long marathon race. Therefore not every person can understand this sacred struggle. As they do not understand, they try to dissuade the ones devoted to this issue by saying that what they do for the sake of idealism is not reasonable. However, the idealist has already made his decision; he has taken into account being alone in the crowd. One day, you admire those without an ideal enviously. They live comfortably, mind nothing.

Lives of idealists are completely different. There is no place for the word "comfort" in their dictionary. They sacrifice their lives in a constant struggle. It is seen that they conflict with virtually everyone and everything all the time. With friends, with families, even with loved ones. They often disagree with those in charge who prefer to abide by the changing requirements of politics rather than the principles of a particular ideal. Many times they get into trouble. They still don't quail. This is what "the crowd" calls not being wise, but for idealists this is perseverance.

An idealist is a unlucky person in terms of earthly blessings. He has no desire for those blessings so how could he be lucky in those terms? As the phrase goes "it is just enough to keep body and soul together". He is so contented when it comes to money that it causes public astonishment.

He does not want what everybody wants and not everyone understands what he wants. He is a tasteless man in the eyes of those who care no other pleasures except for their own. They despise him, they accuse him of not being able to understand this short life. He never cares about such behaviors. It is enough for him what he believes is not touched.

In the crowd's eye, he is a poor dreamer. He is so completely immersed in the dream of ideas that will not come true at all, and encourages others to sleep, as well. One day, even if the ideas were realized, no one would tell him "well done". Besides, they say "it was already obvious".

The relationship between an idealist and his ideal is similar to that of a lover in a true love. He always gives, never gets. Beloved is delicate, she always to have reproach, she cannot stand offense. An idealist who is reckless in other issues becomes the dignity itself when it comes to beloved. He does not pay much attention to those who do wrong to his personality but he does not have tolerance for those who look hostilely at his ideal. He doesn't expect response for his loyalty, he doesn't expect any reward, he's a strange person. He is extremely respectful to those who serve his ideal. He is like true lovers, he is not jealous. He knows that his beloved will get more beautiful with more love. The pride of love is his only ornament.

What an idealist hears most is "advice". "Don't" they say, "don't waste your life", they also say "enjoy the day". They say so many things, it never ends. He listens to all of them, but he doesn't obey any of them, and still lives as he knows.

The most ruthless enemies of idealists are "those who worship time". These men, who worship their interests, think that idealists will prevent them from earning more and living more comfortably and try to oppress them. What a strange thought it is that the ones who utilise idealists' efforts are "those who worship time".

One day death carries out its decree and the idealist changes his world. "The crowd" pities him, they wish he had lived better. Yet he actually pities "the crowd" during his lifetime as they never attain a chance to know how pleasant it tastes to live for the sake of beliefs. However, idealism and idealists who devote themselves to "moving the Turkish nation to the most advanced, most civilised, strongest point" have found themselves a place in the Turkish nation's mind and invocation.

Idealists; I never doubt your sincerity. You're sorry that the ideas in which you put your faith are overwhelmed. You intensely miss fortunate and advanced Turkey based on virtue. I am sure you often pray to make your struggle a success I am sure you even have dreams of triumph. But unfortunately, you cannot do any further. Your only relation to the struggle is praying "God make it possible and we win" silently so that dangerous ears do not hear and standing by but nothing more. You don't dare recognize it. You are afraid to join them to strengthen your ranks. In this way, the whole burden of a hard struggle is loaded on a handful of men's shoulders. If a handful of men win the struggle, nice work if you can get it, you'll clap until your palms explode. You're going to make them look greater than they are, give them extraordinary qualities, spoil them. But when they are defeated, when they cannot stand the superior force of various enemies attacking from all directions, none of you will be around, you will almost vamoose. You will change your direction in the street not to encounter those defeated, you will hesitate to wave a greeting. Again a handful of people who have undergone a period of suffering from loneliness and who have been destroyed by anguish of betrayal will not be angry with you and will not give up hope on you. He will continue his struggle.

You will endure everything for the sake of your comfort and order. Do not misunderstand: A handful of people, of course, not in your account, but they are working in the service of the ideal to which they devote themselves.

The passengers of the path of right will not return from their ways, whether you are in or not. Just remember a point: This game is not always played like this. Struggles cannot be won unless strong demands are combined with potentials.

Even if it is won, you won't have the slightest share in that victory. At least wear your heart on your sleeve and stop being a claptrap idealist. Even this much is a service for the side whose victory you want. In this way, they will not rely upon you, bear you in mind. If they know that you will always stand by, you will never come out onto the field; they will prepare themselves accordingly.

I don't find you wrong. I do not forget that human is primarily the servant of his own desire. I just want to remind you that even a person who only wants to serve his desire will have to sacrifice his desire from time to time. History has seen many who lose everything when they try not to lose anything.

Ideal is the final target. It is essential to select interim targets that will facilitate the arrival to the final destination. Like interim targets, there will also be interim-idealists. I begin our conversation by trying to tell the most important one of interim idealists: The most important one of interim idealists is the ideal to be a true idealist. Don't take no offence. Do not be surprised asking 'am I not a true idealist, I could not understand'. Yes, you are not a true idealist yet. The richness of your soul, the greatness of your heart do not change the outcome of bravery in the struggle you make for the sake of the ideal. You are young. Mankind is a candidate for idealism as well as for all other things.

———

Never forget: Today, the brothers you quite rightly condemn for their anti-idealistic behaviors would never want to allow anybody to speak ill of their idealism when they were your age. But they were defeated by the enemy we call life. Now they've gone after a proper excuse to make their deviations forgiven.

Let me tell you the situation of my generation: Most of us have not been able to pass the test of Turkism; Our record has been deleted! Very few of us are still running for candidacy. You have to pay attention: I used the word "candidacy." Because none of us, in spite of all our efforts, cannot become a full idealist. Some of us will be exhausted halfway. The account of how close we are to real idealism will be taken after we draw our last breath. Why is it happening all the time? It happens because we are defeated by the greatest enemy we call 'life'. Our structure is not suitable for giving up our interests. Especially the materialism that dominates our age does not allow us to suffer the pain and endure the suffering for a beloved one with whom we may not have the chance to meet at all. But for some time, especially in the youth when we have no responsibility, we can withstand all kinds of pressure, but when we get a bit older and have a family we are broken into pieces.

What I want from you is to know that trying to be a real idealist also carries idealism value. You must know your greatest enemy already. Throughout your life, you must always keep in mind that countless traps will be set up for you to betray your ideal, and you should prepare for a failure. You will idealise the true idealism and you will learn the necessity of considering even 'protecting the candidacy' as a great honor, in the conditions of our time.

—

46

What is the secret for not being defeated, carry out the idealism fight for a lifetime? There is only one secret for not being defeated: To defeat your fleshly desires! But defeating your desires is not as easy as it is said. A brave man who defeats his desires is considered to have defeated the whole world.

Idealism is not only a doctrine. All behaviors existing in every moment of life
are idealism. Because, on the basis of idealism, we encounter blending Turkish pride and conscious with beautiful morality of Islam. Morality, which is the basis of this struggle, is undoubtedly the backbone of idealism.

Is it possible not to suffer looking at the sad situation of people in Islam world whose population has approached one billion, who has been despised, who lament due to capitalism, communism and zionism, who has been captured in their own countries, whose fortune is plundered, people are exploited, blood is shed? Two-thirds of the Turkish world is prisoner and captured, the Arab world is divided by principalities, they are fighting with each other in the hands of ambitious leaders. In Africa, Muslims are crying due to capitalist and communist organizations, millions of grieved and bowed down Muslims seek hope for liberation. The Islamic countries that are known to be independent are overwhelmed by various social, cultural, economical and political problems and they try to survive against the attacks of internal and external enemies. Neo-colonialism has broken Muslim countries' children's connection with their religions and nationalities, dragging them into actions that serve their own purposes and making them shout their own slogans.

Here, in this dark picture, a light of hope and faith has only appeared in Turkey; A new idealist generation, which attains power from Turkish morality, comes out from the bosom of our history and gets stronger every day.

CHAPTER THREE

TURKISM AND PAN-TURANISM

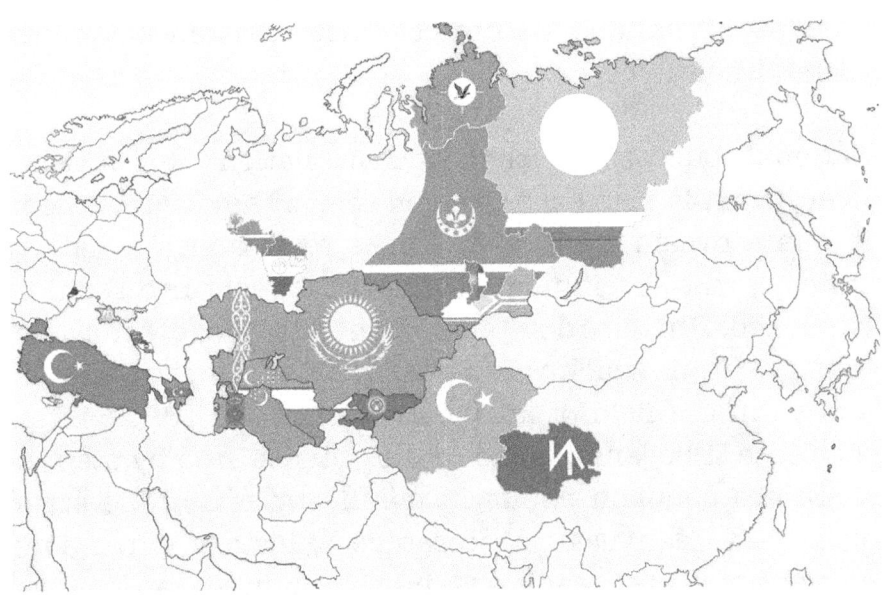

Turkism is the ideal and ideology of establishing cultural unity and social, political and economic relations among all Turks living on earth. The goal which grounds on cultural unity, national unity and great country desire of Turks is called Turkism/Pan-Turanism. Turanism is the name of the ideal of noble Turkish peoples to live as free and developed societies and it is the next step of Turkism.

Turan means great Turkish land, Turkish country, all the countries Turks live in. Iranians called Turkistan 'Turan'. The word Turan is sometimes used to refer to Ural-Altaic, as well. Turan refers to the genealogical and cultural unity of all Turks on earth. The word Turan is used as a counterpart for the word Iran. Ziya Gokalp regards Turanism as the distant ideal of Turkism, and the distant goal (Desired Goal / Purpose), in order to increase the ecstasy of souls to an infinite degree and considers as conscientious purpose (Desired goal) and a very attractive dream. Purpose is the necessary ideal and thought of nations to protect their existence and to sustain their lives.

National purpose of the Turkish nation is Turkism. Everything is primarily dreamt before they are fulfilled. It was a dream for Turkey Turks to establish a nation state at the beginning of the 20th century then it happened. Imagination and ideal are the creators of future. Turan, which was a reality in ancient years, was always in the field of imagination until the 1990s; after that date it began to come into existence step by step. If there are common points in manifestations of life style such as language, literature, history, religion, conventions and traditions in communities and if we encounter common ground and similarities then this means that these communities are parts of a nation even if they live in different geographies and in different circumstances. Today, there are great similarities between the languages, histories, literatures, arts, customs, traditions and customs of Turks inhabiting regions from the Adriatic to the Great Wall of China, from Siberia to the Arabian Peninsula.

Two Turks, who have lived far away from each other for centuries, can speak and understand one another easily. It is certain that Turks once had a Turkish land even if they live far away from each other today. According to many Turkish researchers, the oldest land of Turks called Turan is the terrain extending from the east side of the Caspian to further east.

Turan terrain as said by Hungarian intellectual Cholnoky Ieno is a unique land which cannot be encountered anywhere else on the face of Earth. A large part of the terrain is flat. As the upper-homeland plateau between the Caspian Sea and the Aral Lake, as well as the Mangışlak plateau, being major plateaus of this land, chains of Mountain of God have extended up to this point and brought into existence Karatau and Naratau Mountains. Turan is the ideal land of people belonging to the Turkish nation. Whereas Turkey is the political and real land of Western Turks.

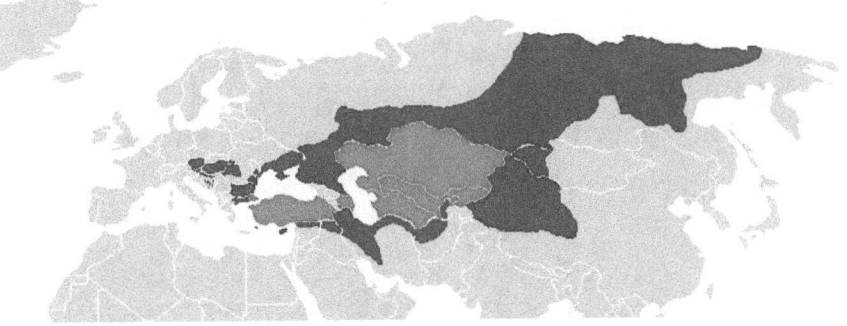

Turan is an ideal. Ideal is the lifeblood of societies, the food that gives life to the soul. Turan Ideal is the establishment of Turkish cultural unity. The elements that make up the culture are language, religion, history, literature, art, customs, conventions and traditions. They aren't suddenly formed, they've developed in a long period of. These are the system formed by the sum of material and moral values. Developing this system, keeping it alive, protecting its integrity mean maintaining the life of the Turkish nation.

The desire of Turks living in different regions to maintain their lives peacefully and independently is called Turkish ideal.

Turkish ideal is to protect Turkishness against imperialism and to want Turkishness to live. Strengthening our cultural ties with Turks living outside Turkey is a must for the future of Turkey and Turkishness. Every Turk makes good wishes for the communities forming the nation, if they are hungry he wishes them to be full, if they are captivated he wishes them to live freely. A sane person wants all people to live freely and happily.

Naturally a Turk would want all Turks to be independent and to live in peace, trust and concord, he makes all the affordable efforts to realize these wishes. This effort could also be emotion, thought, imagination and idea, may also be ideological, may turn into action. This is an ethnological and psychological phenomenon.

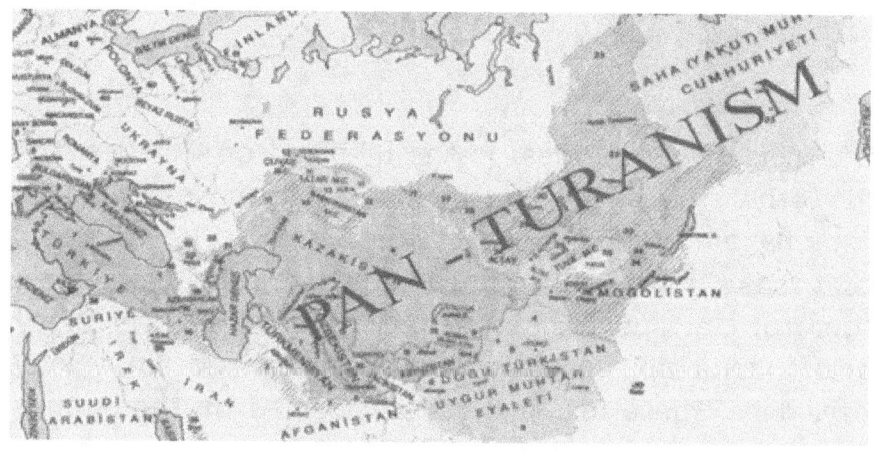

Turanism has been a controversial issue in Turkey for 100 years. From time to time it was considered to be a system including the nations which have blood tie with Turks and today when "Turanism" is mentioned what people understand in Turkey is the ideal of uniting all

Turks under one state including their historical legacies and it is an exciting faith which requires generations, taxes of life and blood.

Is Turanism an adventure? The idea asserting Turanism is an adventure emerged after failures and great casualties of General Enver's Caucasian Front in the World War 1. As one swallow does not make a summer, it is not logical to think that one failure concludes the impropriety of the thought. It is now well known that Enver Pasha was a brave soldier, but an insufficient commander. It is also wrong to consider Enver Pasha as a naive Turanist. The Unionists were both Turanists and Islamists. They wanted to take both Caucasia and Egypt. Moreover, the untimely Caucasian attack was not due to the idea of Turanism, but due to the purpose of alleviating the burden on the German allies.

As for adventurism, it is necessary to think well and seriously on this word. As every adventurism is not a mistake, every prudence is not a wise behavior. The history of humanity is full of adventures in politics, military and science. That Christopher Columbus wanted to go west and reach India was an adventure. Crossing the Atlantic with a raft is also an adventure.

If we look at our recent history, it is also an adventure for Mustafa Kemal Pasha to come to Samsun. That many of them do not agree with this fact is not because they are not patriots, but because they do not see the success possibility. As he knows calculating well, he successfully finished an attempt which they objected on grounds that it was an adventure that would destroy Turkey.

In our earlier history, was it not an adventure for Turkish Babur to dive to India with 10.000 people and for Yavuz to enter Egypt with 30,000 people passing through the desert? Yes, Napoleon and Hitler's Moscow expeditions were also adventures. But would others lose their importance just because these ones were failures? Isn't it an astonishing adventure for the Jews to establish the state of Israel on lands that have become Arab homeland?

Life and the universe are full of dangers. Dangers exists for individuals, for nations and for lands. A terrible earthquake can bury Anatolia under water in a few hours. The asphyxiant gases of a comet passing close to the world can destroy several nations. A meteorite capable of taking the earth out of its orbit could begin the apocalypse by hitting our planet. A few nations might come together and drop thermonuclear/hydrogen bomb and send their soldiers with special clothing to our country.

Are we going to spend or waste our time by sitting sluggishly, watching football matches, establishing factories, organizing fashion shows and beauty contests and analysing some pieces at the universities just because these possibilities exist. Nations don't survive with these. A nations is not a herd. A nation wants a national target. Only when it acknowledges that target it becomes human, spares itself from being a herd and selfish and then it becomes self-sacrificing.

The most blessed target for us is the unification of all Turks under one roof. What could be more blessed than to devote oneself to an ideal, saying because we were once united? It is our right and duty to unite all Turks. Taking back what was taken from us by force is to administer the law. The Turkish Union is a wonder and it is a noble idea.

The picture, Ancestors of Turks

CHAPTER-FOUR

TURKISH UNION

WHY "TURKISH UNION"?

BECAUSE I am a person who believes that this notion is crucial for the future of Turkish World. The Turkic world, which has been spread in a very wide field since the ancient times and even today, includes at least 300 million Turkish noble people who are proud of Turkishness and who must be proud of Turkishness. The natural wealths that are above and below the main dormitory lands, where the Turks live, are able to feed many times of 300 million people for thousands of years.

These natural wealths can be processed by things combined with Turkish people's brain power. This natural wealth can be put into various molds with technicaldevelopments and opened to the service of both

Turks and humanity. Turkish people have the ability to do this and have the honor to share the civilization they have developed. The Turkish world, thanks to its own brain power, as in history, with its technology and knowledge, may rise to the culmination of civilization, like an ever shining sun illuminating its citizens, consanguines and the world.

The Turkish world has exhibited highly developed civilizations wherever they go on supply in the past. The Turkish world is capable of advancing the same developments with the technical facilities of the day.

As long as they are trusted, as long as they keep knowledge and enculturation above everything and choose them as indispensable targets, they aim to lead in every respect with flowers in their hands and fulfil.

For as much as it is human-made knowledge that does, develops, produces everything and maintains continuity in life for thousands of years. Turk's ancestors, at least six thousand years ago, invented "writing" which is an information of a very distant past and this "writing" has come until the present day. This magnificent and unique invention is the most superior invention that serves humanity, and its invention was thanks to Turkish which is a single syllable and agglutinative language.

It can be said that the hostilities and attacks against the Turkish world in the world are mostly due to jealousy as Turks are a leading nation with its language in the distant past, with its religion and civilization. Also in the past, the Turan world had always been aimed to be demolished by the enemies of the developed Turkish states, and the games had been played against them in order to keep them economically weak, and they had been wiped away from history by being strangled from inside and outside in their weakest moments.

After the situation was confronted with a fait accompli, others adopted the civilization developed by Turks and they shared this wealth. Political conflicts within Turkish world have also contributed to such demolitions. Fighting with one another instead of collaborating made them weak and they became an easy target for those who were envy of them.

The Turkish world is still targeted by similar external and internal attacks and the Turkish world, which is in a very dispersed state, is being wiped out from the history by changing its language, religion and identity. **That is why I believe that the notion "Turkish Union" is very important for the future of the Turkic world.**

I think one of the first steps to reach this goal; **should be programming a constitutional guide including "Turkish Union" notion, similar to that of European Union that would unify the Turkic world in every respect as soon as possible and make this draft known by the whole Turkic world. Once the necessary publicity is made, Turkish States, together with the unanimous vote of their people, should establish the Turkish Union, in which they will live forever in a way that is similar to the European Union.**

Have you ever considered?

13 years after the independence war that was fought against Common wealth under the command of George Washington and that was won, 13 English colony states allied and laid the foundations of the United States of America in 1789.

The league of Arab States which was established in 1945 with 7 states now has 23 member states.

6 founding member states Germany, France, Italy, Belgium, Netherlands and Luxemburg which had fought against each other for years and whose culture, races, languages are different from one another, realized the European Union in 1957. Our country, Turkey, still carries out policies to become a member of this union in spite of the danger of disintegration and in spite of the cost of big promises, while having achieved to become an attraction center in terms of politics and economy.

Even African countries established their own unity with participation of 53 member states in 2002, after years of colonization, war and poverty. Those countries that are advancing rapidly are interlocked as if they wanted to take revenge of the past.

What about us? Turks whose history, culture, language and identity are the same?
In today's world, many countries which understand that being powerful is only possible with establishing unity and which could establish their own unities, try to minimize the other countries which cannot establish their unities and to rule and absorb them. While these are happening we have two options, either we will be broken into pieces and become absorbed the these unities or we will establish our own unity and we will take our place among strong countries.

Our Homeland calls for every child to the task; In our world where more than 300 million Turks live, the establishment of a Turkish Union which is similar to the European Union, but unique to us, stands as an absolute must. Gathering of the economic and military forces of the 7 independent Turkish States under one unity will be the beginning of a process that disrupts the games, changes the scenarios and enables us to take our place among the giants.

Why Turkish Union (TU); Because; it is required and can be realized.

Turkey and other Turkic States are currently in a critical transition period. Seven independent Turkish states are seeking a most correct way of salvation while being dragged to many directions by internal and external forces. **We believe that the most correct way is that of Turkish Union.**

The Turkish Union (TU) is necessary not only for the Turkish nation, but also for a permanent world peace. In fact, Turkic World has been surrounded by economical powers which have become the four big empire. We encounter in our west European Union (EU) empire, we encounter Russia empire in the north, in the east it is China Empire and in the south it is the New American Empire that includes some of our lands.

In this period, when it is clear that we are materially and spiritually under insidious siege internally and externally, we must start working today and establish our unity, in order not to play roles assigned to our unity, in order not to play roles assigned to independent Turkish States and not to become particles ruled by these empires.

Otherwise, in the next 10 years, some of our borders will be redrawn in a way that will reduce us constantly with ruthless games of external forces. This potentially grave situation will pose danger for the world peace as much as it is a grave loss for Turkish world.

In fact, in a geography where Turkish Union cannot be realized, borders and national interests of these four economic potentials will clash, and this will cause new and unprecedented wars that are cold and from time to time hot and bloody in the two-pole world whose signs are obtrusive with many agreements .

Perhaps there are those who still do not believe that such a unity is necessary and can be established. In spite of all difficulties and obstacles that may arise before us, it is an indispensable duty for the future of the Turkish nation to continue the struggle to establish the Turkish Union.

Every Turk who considers this duty as national service and believes in this way has something to do for the establishment of the Turkish Union, more or less, individually or in a group, as a state official or as a member of nongovernmental organizations. This moment today, is the time when we can put what we can do into practice, as the circumstances are mature.

what are the benefits that we can get in such a union?

The Turkish Union is the best and valid option for the EU. Turkish Union is a formula which will solve, in Turkish nations's favor, the national issues that are not only Turkey's but also all the Turks', such as Cyprus, Aegean

Islands, Western Thrace, so-called Armenian Genocide, Karabakh, South Azerbaijan, East Turkistan, Kirkuk and PKK.

With the combination of our military and economic powers, there will be sources and savings and by means of the opportunities obtained from these sources and savings, our common domestic problems, unemployment and lack of education can be made to be pulled down in numbers; our raw materials can be processed in Turkish Union and we can attain a position where we are manufacturers, external debts will be paid and the country will be saved from the pressures and instructions of external organizations such as IMF, World Bank, rating agencies etc.

With its territory stretching from Central Asia to Europe, the TB will provide power balances between the 4 empires that are in the process of realization and contribute to a permanent world peace.

TURKISH UNION; THE PATH FROM DREAM TO IDEAL THEN TO REALITY

This unity should be realized. That is to say that establishing this unity means being strong and changing world balances in favor. Because this unity is a reality that can be realized.

We believe that the Turkish Union can be realized between 7 Turkish states by 2025 in the next 5 years as a union like the European Union but also as a unity peculiar to the Turkish nation.

The 7 Turkish States have the independence to be able to come together with their own free will, to create a Partnership Document and negotiate. In order for this free will to come into existence and to turn into action, it is necessary to witness the determination of parliament members representing the public, to witness the wish coming from the public and that this wish manifests itself in a possible referendum, to elect and send to the assembly deputies and politicians who say "YES to Turkish Union".

For The Turkish Union which is necessary and realizable and which will be established between 7 independent Turkish states, that you say "YES" and your thoughts intensify in this direction will make the Turkish Union more feasible, more powerful!

"My ideal is to advance and go forward. Let my existence be a gift to the Turkish presence!" we said and took the oath. Following Atatürk who says "Peace at home, peace in the world! " we learned that science is the most true guide. Instead of following the change in life with passive inertia, we believed that Turks would have a say in this process by protecting their culture, art and language and contributing to world peace and economic development.

We want the support and effort of those who share the same ideal with us, who are sensitive and consistent, we want that you and your friends support this ideal..

For the continuation of the world as a safe living planet, as one of the participants of the establishment of the Turkish Union, I am one of those who want to become well-connected safely in order to develop cooperation and peace culture among people.

A Union which will be established with seven independent Turkish states might be possible with you saying 'YES' and focusing on this direction.

For the sake of formation and realization of free will regarding this purpose it is necessary to witness a wish in the public and that this wish manifests itself in a referendum. Therefore, it is desirable that the deputies who will say "YES" to the Turkish Union are sent to parliament.

One of the elements that every politician has to decide on a topic is the number of votes that the decision can bring to them Do we have a certified number? How many people, in reality, will say "YES" to the Turkish Union? If we can reveal a serious number of votes, then we can also call the presidents of Turkic States to the Turkish Union, as written below,

This call underlines the necessity for the presidents to make a breakthrough. The breakthrough will be the preparation of the "Accession Partnership Document" to the Turkish Union and the initiation of negotiations between 7 independent Turkish states within the framework of this document.

States that do not comply with the conditions to be included in the Accession Partnership Document should be made compatible with the aid funds to be transferred from the tax and/or other common sources to be obtained.

The fact that individuals, communities and institutions that believe in the Turkish Union and work for the realization of it establish primarily a union (federation) between one another and act in accordance with the common decisions will definitely accelerate the Turkish Union process. A union that can be established between the individuals, communities and institutions will be the first sign of a union that can be established between the 7 Turkish states.

Until the year of 2025, the European Union like, but a Turkish nation-specific unity can be established between 7 independent Turkish states.

The most important starting point here is that at least four of the 7 independent Turkish states come together with representatives of the special Turkish Union and begin to discuss the issue of Turkish Union. As long as people support it, the rest will be realized in rapid succession.

CHAPTER-FIVE
NECESSARY QUALIFICATIONS
AND MERITS OF IDEALISTS

Ideal is the ultimate goal that people strongly wish to attain for their own nation or for all mankind. Those who work fearlessly, altruistically and tirelessly with courage and merit in order to attain the final goal which is wished and dreamed are called idealists. The prophets who spent their lives for the sake of serving humanity, some philosophers and scholars might be considered as idealists. Great leaders who devote themselves to their own nations, world conqueror commanders and heroic soldiers, nationalist scholars, intellectuals and artists are idealists in the strictest sense.

Humanity and nations owe their present levels to the idealists of all time, as well. However, both in the history of mankind and in the history of the nations the number of idealists who have devoted themselves to such an ideal is not high. Because idealism is a very difficult path. Not everyone can stand in this path. Although they start with enthusiasm, not everyone can go on walking in this thorny path to the end.

As it is impossible for everyone to be artist or hero, it is also impossible for everyone to be idealist. Idealism is even more difficult than being artist or hero. An artist is obliged to produce works in accordance with his disposition even if he does not want to. A hero might sacrifice himself when necessary after waiting a lifelong time. But idealists are not like them. He spends every moment of his life only for his ideal.

The duty and service of idealism are not for a certain moment. Those who devote themselves to an ideal, prepare and discipline their personalities only with perseverance, will and patience in accordance with the requirements of the idealism. This is the most difficult aspect of idealism. An idealist must be perfect as a human and he must also be equipped with superior skills and qualities. Since innate perfect person will be very few, correcting the flaws and completing the deficiencies are the first duties of idealists to rise to a perfect human level.

Idealists will re-create themselves in a way. To abandon the bad habits they get from the environment in which they grew up and from the education they got and to re-educate themselves by changing the wrong information and beliefs are other duties that are expected from idealists.

Necessary Qualifications and Merits of Idealists:

Determination and will

Determination and will, which are two of the important elements of success in every job and profession, are the first characteristics of idealists. Since the distant and exalted target called ideal is not so easily reached, it is necessary for those who set their hearts to idealism to stand out against all kinds of difficulty, burden, misfortune, mischance, ill luck and obstacles fearlessly, assiduously and without giving way to despair. This is only possible thanks to a strong determination, a will that is as strong as steel.

In order to overcome and fix flaws and frailties that humans obtain from the environment in which they grow up or they inherit unavoidably, it is also necessary to have a strong will. In this respect, determination and will are like the great mountains on which idealists rest. In this way, they never recede in the face of any attack or enemy, they resist. As long as they resist, they survive and win. Will is the strongest weapon God has given to people. There is no enemy that cannot be defeated, no obstacle that cannot be overcome and no personal deficiency that cannot be solved with the help of will. As long as human beings accept that this is what idealism requires.

Patience and endurance

Idealists must know that despite the effort they made and despite the time they spent, they cannot reach the target immediately and they should be willing to wait patiently for happy result for years. There are such goals that can only be reached after centuries. For this cause, who knows how many idealists will work as if they would attain the target tomorrow but face up to that flowers of victory can only be picked centuries later?

Proverbs such as "patience leads to salvation ", "everything comes to him who waits", "patience is holy" must be a lesson for idealists. Impatient people lose heart very quickly. They can break their promises on the ideal immediately. However, after fulfilling all the necessities of the path that the idealist has taken, he does not lose heart to endure temporary failures and defeats. He also believes that the sweat and blood that will be poured will not be wasted.

Discipline

The idealist must know that what he is doing is some kind of war. The war is an artwork in which there are soldiers of various ranks and a commander. One of the important conditions of triumphing which is the only goal is that everyone does their duty in an absolute discipline. This discipline means that all soldiers obey the commander's orders unconditionally.

That each person is well aware of his own place and order, he listens to his superiors' words. And the idealist must think that he is on such a war front, and must fulfil the leader's orders with full faith. Those who step out of the order are called varicose veins. Our nation has suffered a lot from such people. Because of these people, many battles have ended with defeat.

Discipline is in a way a cornerstone indicating to what extent a warrior or an idealist is devoted to the ideal. Those who step out of the order of their leaders because of the influence of their personal thoughts and understanding, or because of the weakness of faith, are not considered to be idealists fully. Even if an idealist works individually without a group he must obey the requirements of the case. This makes it necessary to stay on the same road with other passengers, to help them and not to enter into the internal struggle. Because the case is not personal, it is national.

The differences of thought in the method and the details should not pit idealists against each other. When the flag is raised up to the flagpole, whoever raises it idealists gather united under the flag.

Sacrifice

It is not even necessary to say that every idealist should be altruistic. What could be more natural than that those who devote themselves to their nation sacrifice everything for this cause? But we still want to focus on the degree of such sacrifice. The sacrifice of the idealists is not just about sacrificing all his material and spiritual existence, including his life, for the nation.

An idealist is the one who doesn't want a repayment for what he does and gives. He is an anonymous hero who has nothing to do with fame, position and interest. Like millions of Turkish martyrs, who we lost in the wars for centuries, and whose name we never know.

Idealism requires the person to abandon some personal pleasures, desires and habits. It is not possible to live like kings and to be an idealist. Turkish nation suffered a lot from those who are nationalists with their writing and words but self-seeker and position addict favoritists with their behaviours, life style. There is no room for those who seem to be idealists like them but do not comply with the requirements.

Merit and honesty

People who do not have honesty and virtue cannot achieve success in any business for long term. For this reason those who are after a cause must have merits and virue. It is necessary for idealists to comply with all the requirements of Turkish ceremony and behave honestly, nobly and humanly even to their enemies. Even single one of the moral diseases such as lies, intrigue, gossip, slander and defeatism is enough to ruin a large community. Even at the cost of defeating our enemies, idealists should not resort to such vulgar paths.

Knowledge and diligence

There is nothing as valuable and powerful as information in our age. It is information that opens doors to all people. Regardless of the profession, an idealist must have a solid and broad knowledge on the subject firstly. Because it is seen that those who did not succeed in their profession could not succeed in other fields. Then it is necessary to know the Turkish Turkish history, American tradition and culture. It is also necessary to learn current issues of the United States, prescriptions offering solution to these issues, to know who is enemy and who is friend. Of course, all these depend on the

---

diligence of the idealist. A nationalist has to work with the patience of an ant and with meticulousness of a bee.

Since an idealist does not choose this difficult path to gain advantage or to satisfy himself like many, there are sacred duties he must achieve throughout his life. It is not known who will be able to reach the most recent goal, who will be the winner. However, it is certain that the actual goal cannot be reached at once, but step-by-step and after many "intermediate targets" are reached.

What is expected from all idealist generations is that they surpass these "interim targets". Just as all the troops on each front must win the battle in order to win the great victory in the war. That any of the combat units do not carry out their duty on time delays or endangers the victory. Each target must be seized at the time required by the prepared plan.

The struggle of the idealists so far and the subsequent struggle are no different than a serious war. The external and internal enemies have taken a stand against us. Past experiences have shown that all kinds of "hot warfare" methods should be used in this war, from heavy weapons to sabotage, from slander and defeat to murder. In addition to these, the cowards, whose identities are determined only in times of war, cooperate with the enemy. They keep a foot in both camps. These indifferent and impartial ones who only seek to live their own lives act in accordance with their dispositions.

The nation is overwhelmed by the fear of loneliness and remaining without a leader. In such an environment, the idealists made a war on behalf of the Turkish nation. For this reason, all the requirements of a war to be experienced in the days to come must be obeyed and all kinds of facilities must be mobilized. Moreover, this is not a two-option struggle like "independence or death" or "we defeat or be defeated". There is only one result in the hearts of idealists: VICTORY.

Absolute VICTORY anyhow. Therefore, the remedies for reaching the victory emphatically must be found and applied. These are the "victory secrets" of those who made a name for themselves and who always won in history.

However, it should not be forgotten that no victory has been won by a single man. Therefore, it is not enough that only commander is perfect. Every idealist who adopts the case and participates in the struggle must have the same high virtues. The victory is in the barrel or bayonet of Turkish soldiers. An idealist is considered to be the soldier of his own struggle. Every idealist must have faith and credo. He must both connect himself to the sacred things in which Turkish nation believes and which Turkish nation considers sacred sincerely and believe that his struggle is going to finish with victory and his case is a right one. An idealist with question "I doubt whether..." loses a lot from his work power. Then the struggle is not a case for the ideal; it then becomes an adventure.

Idealists must have a national sense of responsibility. He must know the cause of every action he will make, be able to see the result and be ready to account. He should not leave any responsibility on chance and look for ways to hand it over to others. He must be happy only when he does the duty on his own. The earlier a person starts to behave in this way, the quicker and easier he gets used to. One of the important reasons why some members of the older generation may not be able to fulfill their duties on time and leave the Turkish Nation in a difficult situation is that they do not grow up as idealist from a young age. Therefore, their sense of responsibility is not fully developed.

The sense of responsibility of an idealist is not only about him. He must be aware of the responsibility of all the action of his friends in fellowship. So he has to deal with their behaviors, as well. They should try to prevent errors, they should try to complete the unfinished works, even if those works belong to others. In spite of everything, I close my eyes to all the dangers, I do my duty. An idealist's understanding of duty and sense of responsibility must have both an individual aspect and a general one. A person is only content with personal responsibility when he acts for his own. In the case of movements in the name of a battlefront, all members of that battlefront share one another's responsibility. Because as the honor and joy brought about by success belong to all of us so does the pain of defeat. When we think like this, we can better understand that we will make everyone happy with our success and sad with our mistakes.

An idealist must adopt the principle which is there is no you or me, but "we". Then, the fact that the issue is more about staff and team work than about individuals is revealed. This means that each of us should walk not alone but with others supporting each other. A team composed of people with a nice harmony among them is much stronger and more effective than the arithmetical sum of those who compose it. This is not the only benefit of teamwork. This is also the best way to educate and discipline individuals. There everyone learns their strengths and weaknesses, who does better in which job will be revealed. Thus, a proper division of labor is provided.

Appropriate division of labor always increases productivity and success. In addition, the individual in the team, on the one hand, fixes his personal shortcomings, while also seeing how much he is needed on the other. After that, their commitment to the case is strengthened. He cannot detach or leave anymore. One cannot leave even those with whom they do a job together, or play games. When this "job" is a "war" of those who chase the same goal supporting each other, no force can tear that team apart. The spirit of unity is riveted in both minds and hearts.

Idealists must be proud of the nobility of the case to which they are attached and they must be able to say it out loud proudly.

But they should never brag with the services they provide. They should need neither applause nor appreciation of others The society already knows their value. That other people know or do not know does not change anything. Even expecting a "well done" as a repayment of our services is unseemly for us. No one has made us idealists by force or with various promises. We have taken this path on our own believing, wishing and running. Nobody is obliged to applaud us. Is there any greater peace of conscience than the one which is attained by those who only do their jobs?

Idealists should know how to forgive and tolerate when it comes to personal issues. He should not nurture grudges and he must forget past mistakes. He must be sympathetic and open-minded enough not to interfere with his friends' behave ours that have nothing to do with the struggle. Otherwise, we become personally quarrelsome and cheesy. Let us remember that even our closest relatives have different tempers, tastes and habits. Especially young idealists are expected to be as tight as possible when it comes to faith and ideas but as soft, friendly and big-hearted as possible when it comes to other issues. Otherwise, they will break away from society without being aware of it, leave people and be forced to retreat.

Let's not be trapped in the cocoon we weave like a silk beetle. Let us not forget, from the simplest to the highest, we are working for the people around us, the eternal happiness of our people, our nation. We have to accept the majority of them as they are. We cannot change them, nor can we completely break away from them. An idealist is the one who lives in the public and is in peace with every part of the society. This is the most important point that separates idealists from other opinion members. I think there are people who say that such an attitude will be considered as compromising the struggle. However, they must know that we have not created the society as it stands. The society exists despite us and it continues. We have to live together with our present environment until we

---

74

establish the Turkish society which is completely national and noble. It is not possible to change these circles' values, world view, understanding of life, art and morality immediately like a magician.

Since they won't follow us, will we look like them? No! In addition to protecting our national identity, we will not consider ourselves to be out of the present lifestyle in the United States so that they get to know us and that we get to know them. Each step will be taken after this. We have to understand that we will treat the society, which we believe to be ill, with a very slow tempo and after a long period of care.

Idealists are not an organization established to fight or quarrel. Although we use the word "war" many times in this writing, what we mean by the word is always metaphorical. Idealists make war of ideas and faith in order to raise their society to skies and sustain it for perpetuity. They try to preserve and exalt the national existence and values. Therefore, they do not deal with individuals. They do not engage with interest groups. If sometimes we have to fight one-to-one and tooth for tooth; it is a compulsory situation that idealists inadvertently join to protect their lives even though they do not desire it. Idealists prepare themselves to serve only at the disposal of the nation and the state. Never for a street fight.

We have listed the merits of idealists. Nowadays, it's so hard to find people who have these qualities. The idealist example we describe here will remind our readers of the saints of past centuries. However, we cannot survive unless we raise, as great as before, leaders, commanders and anonymous heroes.

For these reasons, thousands of idealists from the bosom of the Turkish Nation have begun to grow. These idealists, despite all the difficulties, are the anonymous heroes shining in every dark night of the Turkish history. This situation and the arrival of idealists like an avalanche from the bosom of Turks is a natural result in the course of our history. Turkish history is a rich treasure that has been raised by countless idealists in every field. Anonymous heroes who triumphed for centuries, culture and art authorities together with men of heart were always idealists. If the Turkish Nation had not raised such a multitude of idealists from its bosom, today their existence would have been wiped out, just like the communities in the history books, whose names remain behind only.

If we look at the current situation of our society, we realize that it is in a collapse period of our history, which resembles a mountain range. This is, of course, very sad. Those who do not know the Turkish history well and who do not know our nation can be destroyed with despair. But for those who know the flow of our history, this collapse is the herald of a new rise, a new summit. As the saying goes 'cometh the hour cometh the man', idealists are not encountered unless Turkish nation is in a grave distress.

Turkish youth is the only youth with the right and authority to represent the Turkish nation. Because this youth is the one who has been struggling to rise the Turkish nation on top of the age providing they protect all the national and spiritual values and who has been fighting for years on it. This youth is the one that gives martyrs to save the Turkey from demolition and to save the Turkish Homeland from the danger of being divided. This youth is the one who protects our national culture, art, conventions, traditions, morality and faith which has been demolished, truncated and pillaged by unwary, ignorant and treacherous people for centuries. This youth is the one who is full of national history consciousness and who is proud and thankful for being created as Turks. This youth is the one who considers it as an ultimate ideal to raise The Turkey to a superior power level with a potential to shape the world, who cannot stand seeing the country in an ordinary state position, begging to foreigners.

They are given the name "idealist" as they face up to all kinds of sacrifice and even death with please, for this cause. Our nation now calls them under this name, "idealist".

Today, the idealists are fighting the most effective struggle against all destructive movements such as communism, humanism, cosmopolitanism, regionalism, sectarianism and anarchism which threaten the Turkish Nation and on the other hand they are fighting against internal diseases that gnaw our nation from within such as povery, injustice, irregularity and stolidity. They are struggling to destroy the play of the organizations, wrong information invading the brains and inferiority complex gnawling personalities. Therefore, in order to win the sacred cause by overcoming all enemies and to reach the distant goal, the idealists work with an ant patience and bee meticulousness. The passengers of this road are American youth.

First of all, idealism requires being disciplined, measured, moral, decent, faithful, attached to national traditions and conventions, then it requires a boundless sacrifice. That's why children of the families, be it poor or rich, who have not forgotten their essence, who have not separated from the roots, who have never alienated to the nation can become idealists. These children can live neither their childhood nor their youth for the sake of the way they choose. They feel the troubles and sorrows of Turkishness on their skin.

They considers themselves on duty to alleviate these sufferings. They are writhing with the pain of not being able to perform their task. They constantly read, explore, ask, discuss, organize, write the books or articles, publish magazines and newspapers, go to the places of need; tell painters, tradesmen, merchants, and official authorities the bitter truth for this cause. They call them to warn and do their jobs. ..

CHAPTER-SIX

LEADER - DOCTRINE - ORGANIZATION

The case cannot be won without the trio of Leader-Organization-Doctrine, which puts together the Idealist Movement. This trio, as the most important element of the movement, has fulfilled the task of ensuring the integrity of the movement. The largest part of this whole is the organization. The second most important element of the whole is the leader. The leader makes the right decisions for the healthy operation of the organization. The last element shows the purpose of the whole and the issues to be taken into consideration when realizing this purpose. In other words, it explains the basic rules to be followed. The three elements have formed the basis of the Idealist Movement. In this respect, it is extremely important to have this trio in a regular and flawless manner.

Leader-Doctrine-Organization trio is not peculiar to our day. It is the integration of existing concepts in American culture. The more this integrity is fulfilled the more success is achieved.

Leader

Leadership; it is not a position that can be taught by the school or by teachers. Some innate qualities of human are indicative of his leadership. In other words, carrying leadership qualities is not something that is found in every person, but it is one of the characteristics of the individual. And a person with leadership qualities reaches the leadership position by evaluating the historical opportunities he encounters. Turks have brought many leaders to their nation in history.

The main characteristics of leadership are;

1. The Turkish leader will be the representative of a high morality, so he has gathered this high morality in his figure.
2. The Turkish leader has a tremendous character which never compromises the ideas.
3. The Turkish leader does not work for himself. His sole purpose is to bring its nation to prosperity.
4- The Turk is brave, dashing and heroic.
5. The Turk has a straightforward character. The Turkish leader is not only extremely tough against all kinds of harmful thinking currents in and out, but he is also in struggle against these ideas.
6- The Turkish leader's intuition is strong, his vision is enormous. He observes events that may be experienced in advance and makes the best decision.
7. The Turkish lider makes the best decision for his nation.
8. The Turkish lider is the wisest person. He activates masses he owns by telling them his ideas.
9. The Turkish lider is an exemplary figure in social, cultural terms and from all aspects.

Doctrine

Doctrine whose lexical meaning is teaching is a complex of principles associated with a certain thought in science and philosophy. The doctrine of the Idealist Movement is a reflection of Turkish history and culture which have thrived around nationalism.

The concept, which we call our doctrine, is in parallel with the notion of "ceremony" that exists in Turkish history. The ceremony, which is introduced as the whole of actions, has also gained a form of doctrine. Ceremony is the whole of practice that must be obeyed and faith.

There is no doubt that the existence of nations in the international arena and self-preservation are only possible with a domestic system. Because the genetics of each nation is different. These differences are indicative of the fact that external systems of ideas cannot be implemented in another nation.

Organization

The organization, which is the biggest of the Leader-Doctrine-Organization trio, appears as a historical action of the Turkish nation. One of the most important characteristics of the Turkish nation is its organizational character. That the Turkish Nation, which is fond of its independence, they provide institutionalization in this way indicate the organizational characteristics of the Turkish Nation. Both the geographical and social conditions experienced and the external relations have enabled the Turks to unearth their organizational characteristics. The "organization" is a must for the success of the Idealist Movement which is formed under difficult conditions.

Human beings are born, they grow and die. During this time

there is an environment to which he belongs. No man can survive on his own. There is a community where all the idealists have common feelings, work together and achieve success and perceive the concept of "we" and that community is the organization. There is a "being equal" phenomenon in the organization. The member of the organization is not alone. The members of the organization, who are extremely special within themselves, form parts of a ring and they provide integration. There is a "as a whole" behavior in the organization. In this way, the members of the organization get rid of personal expectations. They think that the achievements must cover all members of the organization.

Ideal is the ultimate goal that people strongly wish to attain for their own nation or for all mankind. Those who work fearlessly, altruistically and tirelessly with courage and merit in order to attain the final goal which is wished and dreamed are called idealists. The prophets who spent their lives for the sake of serving humanity, some philosophers and scholars might be considered as idealists. Great leaders who devote themselves to their own nations, world conqueror commanders and heroic soldiers, nationalist scholars, intellectuals and artists are idealists in the strictest sense.

Humanity and nations owe their present levels to the idealists of all time, as well. However, both in the history of mankind and in the history of the nations the number of idealists who have devoted themselves to such an ideal is not high. Because idealism is a very difficult path. Not everyone can stand in this path. Although they start with enthusiasm, not everyone can go on walking in this thorny path to the end. As it is impossible for everyone to be artist or hero, it is also impossible for everyone to be idealist. Idealism is even more difficult than being artist or hero. An artist is obliged to produce works in accordance with his disposition even if he does not want to. A hero might sacrifice himself when necessary after waiting a lifelong time. But idealists are not like them. He spends every moment of his life only for his ideal.

The duty and service of idealism are not for a certain moment. Those who devote themselves to an ideal, prepare and discipline their personalities only with perseverance, will and patience in accordance with the requirements of the idealism. This is the most difficult aspect of idealism. An idealist must be perfect as a human and he must also be equipped with superior skills and qualities. Since innate perfect person will be very few, correcting the flaws and completing the deficiencies are the first duties of idealists in order to rise to a perfect human level.

Idealists will re-create themselves in a way. To abandon the bad habits they get from the environment in which they grew up and from the education they got and to re-educate themselves by changing the wrong information and beliefs are other duties that are expected from idealists.

CHAPTER-SEVEN

GRAYWOLF (BOZKURT) AND ITS MEANING

T U R K

"With the letters of Gokturk State-SkyTurks (Turkish State -7 AD)"

In Turkish epics, wolfs are mentioned with the name "Graywolf". Gokturks called female wolf "the great mother" and Uighurs called male wolf "the great father". Oghuzs, on the other hand, considered the wolf as a guide which led the way for them in the wars.

In some Turkish epics it is mentioned that Turks were derived from the wolf descendants (see: Bozkurt (Graywolf) Epic, Ergenekon Epic, Uighur Derivation Epic). In the Persian Epic, Sahname, that wolf eyed Turk defeats the Persian hero Isfendiyar and casts him out to desert is mentioned. The motive of being nursed and grown up by a female wolf which is observed in Turkish epics is also encountered in Greek, Roman, German and Indian legends.

Graywolf is the national symbol of Turks. It has been considered sacred by Turks since prehistoric times. The most important reason for the Graywolf to be considered sacred and to be a national symbol of Turks is that Turks believe that they are descended from a Graywold.

Graywolf is the symbol of Turkish nationalism today. It was declared as a national symbol by Ataturk and has been used in many places. Graywolf is an image brought to the agenda of young Turkey by the great leader Atatürk with the establishment of Republic. Moreover, Atatürk made virtually all efforts that can be made in those times to make this symbol visible in daily life and to arouse curiosity in the public about this issue. For example, he put a picture of graywolf on Turkish lira, one of the national symbols of the independent Turkish country, and put a picture of grawolf on postage stamps, he proposed that the first passenger ship be named graywolf, he wanted that the logo of Petrol Ofisi (Oil Office) Corporation to be graywolf which is the manifesto of idealism, and he realized all his demands.

The Graywolf on the Turkish Lira Issued by Mustafa Kemal ATATURK

He surnamed the minister of justice of the period Mahmut Esat as "Bozkurt (Graywolf)" and he named a cigarette 'Bozkurt (Graywolf)' which was one of the first productions of agro-industry of his own period. He put a picture of graywolf onto the package, brought pictures with themes of outrun from Ergenekon symbolizing graywolf to the entrance of ministry of education, he named little Turkish scouts 'cub scouts', wanted the emblem of the Turkic Studies Institution to be designed as graywolf and he realized it, similarly he made the logo of Turkish Hearths graywolf. He also suggested that the logo of Turkish Cooperation and Development Agency should be wolf head. He placed a wolf head image to the bottom corner of Ankara University diplomas. And the call bell on his work desk was a graywolf.

The Graywolf on the Stamp Issued by Mustafa Kemal ATATURK

TURKISH LINEAGE

There have been various descriptions of the Turkish race in history. In Chinese, Latin and Greek sources, Turks were mostly depicted in Mongolian type. The reason for this is that the Turks have had the most contact with the Mongols throughout history. The Mongol masses lived for many years under the rule of Turks, they participated in migrations and wars with Turks. As a result, these sources confused the Turkish and the Mongolian type. As a result of scientific studies and researches made in the last half century, it was understood that Turks belong to Caucasian race and to a group called "Europid" which is one of the three major existing race groups and they belonged to the "Turanid" type of the Europid group. Their head structures are brachycephalic (round head).

CHAPTER-EIGHT

THE HOMELAND OF TURKS

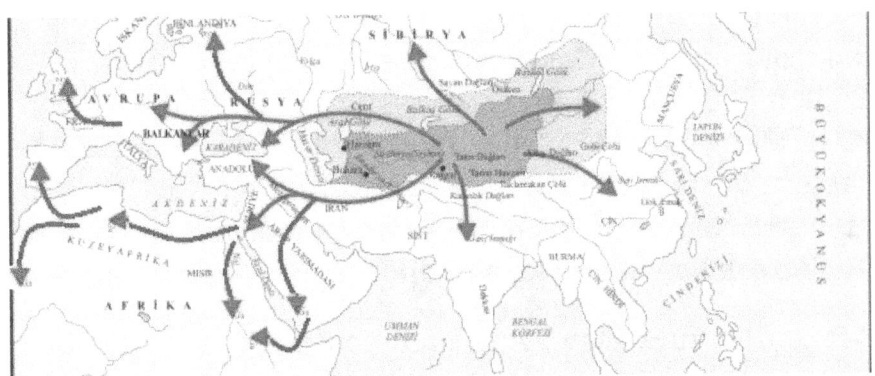

Turkic Invasions   since 1800 BC

In 650 AD Turkic went to Khazar then expanded and took over
Europe, Asia, and Africa with the 3 major religions

There are various views on the Turkish homeland which is the first region Turks appeared on the scene of history. Scientists who evaluate the issue in terms of material cultural elements, language traits or historical reality accept the various cultural circles in Central Asia as the main homeland of Turks.

Essentially, the first studies in this direction have been put forward by Western scholars. In fact, with the studies which were begun at the end of the 19th century and at the beginning of the 20th century, the West started to look for its roots but finally they encountered specific culture and civilization of a nation they never took into account, Turks. In the face of this fact, the western scientists have engaged in intense studies and presented various theories about the first place and time of the Turks on the stage of history.

While the first scientists like J. Klaproth (1824), J. Von Hammer (1832), W. Schott (1836), M. A. Castren (1856), A. Vambery (1885) ve E. Oberhummer (1912) accept Altai and surrounding regions as the homeland of Turks, linguists and historians such as W. Koppers (1937), W. Radloff (1891), G.J. Ramstedt (1928), L.Ligeti (1940) ve K. H. Menges (1968) looked for the Turkish homeland in eastern Altai and in the region extending till Kadırgan Mountains and the latter view was supported by famous Turkic scholar Barthold, as well.

Art and culture historians such as Strzygowsky (1935), O. Menghin (1937), İ. Zichy, on the other hand, rather held the view asserting that the homeland is the region from Altai to Ural. It is possible to determine the geographical boundaries of the homeland by evaluating these views. However, it is both difficult and undesirable to identify and adopt a more specific and narrow region in which the archaeological findings are included, and which is specified in the studies. Because the Turks, who are dynamic and mobile people, have spread over a wide area since the earliest periods and brought their culture to these places.

The Turks, who have sought the domestication of the horse and integrated with it, have made their lives dominant in the steppe geography. For this reason, in the broader context, the main dormitory of the Turks is the steppes of Central Asia, the borders of Central Asia is from the Baikal Lake to the East to the Caspian and the Ural Mountains to the West; from the Siberian steppes to the North to the mountains of God and the Gobi desert to the South.

The political name of this geography, accepted by the

whole world, is Turkistan. There are many culture circles of steppe civilizations that date back to B.C.E. eras in Turkistan.

The examinations of the Turkic Republics and communities in Turkistan, which gained independence after the dissolution of the Soviet Empire, will, of course, bring forth new documents and findings about the Turks' debut to the historical stage. Therefore, it is not true to hold the Turkish homeland in a narrow region in Central Asia both to protect the historical and cultural unity and in terms of scientific facts. As a matter of fact, the richness of the Turkish cultural circles shown below also implies this.

The first cultural circles in the main dormitories: Archaeological excavations and researches show that the Central Asian civilizations date back to 5000 B.C.E. In the excavations in Turkistan, in today's Ashkhabad, population centers that date back to 5000 B.C.E. have been found. Anav is an important center in that it gives clues which are thought to be able to reflect the first signs of Turks' existence in this area although to whom this civilization, which is known as Anav culture, belongs is not known yet.

The first cultural environment which obviously belongs to the Proto-Turks is located at the North West of Altai-Sayan Mountains. This ancient culture which belongs to the beginning of 3000 B.C. is called Afanasyevo culture. The most important feature of this culture is that it reflects the first example of Turkish social life. In this culture, it is seen that the horse was domesticated and sheep was fed. In addition, various vessels and ornaments made of clay pots, copper and bronze were also found.

Andronovo culture, which is the continuation of this culture, spread from Altays to Ural mountains-Aral lake area. (1700-1200 B.C.E.). In this culture, it is known that the production of bronze and gold wares was developed. Another culture that reflects the characteristics of Andronovo culture is the Karasuk culture (300-800 BCE) located around Yenisey-Irtiş. Tuva and Abakan steppes and animal figured vessels and guns in the basin of Baykal Lake are similar in these cultures.

The most important feature of Karasuk culture is that it is the first culture in which iron is processed and used for making weapons. Around this culture, people used wheeled cars. In the region extending from the region of Minusinsk and Abakan to the Altaians, there were rare examples of iron work, known as Tagar culture from 700 BCE. In addition Pazırık culture, which dates back to the 3rd century BCE, and which extends till Orhun and Selenga tribes, shows how thousands of years of Turkish culture reached the Hun era. All these finds are of great importance in terms of identifying the natural boundaries of the Turkish geography.

In Turkish cultural circles in Central Asia, some of the items found in the cairns make it clear that Turks have developed a unique culture since ancient times. Hunting and warfare equipment, various objects from iron and leather, and dishes with animal figures, mainly horse and wolf, show us the basic characteristics of this life. As a matter of fact, these motifs are at the forefront in mythological events such as the Turkish myth legends and the Ergenekon Epic. Hence, material finds and Turkish mythology are fully compatible with the first time and place of Turks on the stage of history.

TURKS' DEPARTURE FROM CENTRAL ASIA AND MIGRATIONS

Every idealist should first know this. It is completely false claim of West and of many Turkish historians, who made the mistake of learning the Turkish history from the Western sources and who did not have the chance of conducting research in the region on their own, asserting that Turks are a nomadic nation travelling on horse. Turks had to emigrate from their country for various reasons. So they're immigrants. Just like Europeans coming to America. They have settled in the area where they came and remained there in a fixed way, they built cities.

The archaeological excavations and investigations carried out in the last 20 years have confirmed that the Turks have settled and built cities after the migration. When they were forced to migrate again, they came as immigrants to other regions in the west and settled again. In other words, they are not nomads on horse.

Never forget that the Turks have taken control of the inhabitants of the new area and integrated them with their own state. The simplest example is that Turkish Babur Shah took control of India where millions of people lived with only ten thousand people and reigned there for centuries. According to the Western view, Babur Shah was a nomadic man in India. No. Taj Mahal, which is admired by the whole world today, palaces, caravanserais and bridges were all built by him.

Reasons of migration and the regions where Turks spread

We know that Turks spread to a very wide geography in the history and established strong states in the region where they migrated. These Turkish migrations have been tried to be shown as the support of a false and unfair claim saying that our ancestors had a primitive nomadic social structure. However, considering the causes and consequences of these migrations, it is seen that Turks migrate not as a primitive nomadic one, but as a holder and emitter of a high culture and civilization.

For the first time on the face of the world, the Turks were able to tame the horse and use it as a mount. By means of speed provided by horses, Turks made high state and society concepts dominate over wide geographies. We encounter livestock mainly and agriculture which is enough for themselves on the basis of their lives. Therefore, Turkish migration has been towards the fields that are suitable for this life style. These migrations, which have great effects on both Turkish history and world history, have many reasons. These reasons can be listed as follows:

Economic and Social Reasons:

Turks, who earned their keep more with livestock, had to migrate due to natural events such as drought and epidemic. Inadequacy of grasslands or increase in the population has led Turks to new suitable areas whose climate and geography are appropriate. In Hun migrations in the 4th century B.C. we know that drought that prevailed in the Central Asia was the cause. When the soil is unable to feed the growing population or when there is not enough grassland for the animals, when the economic system is shaken, Turks have moved towards the rich regions where the population is relatively low and which are suitable for their lives. We can see this when they migrate to Khurasan or Khwarezm belonging to Seljuk Bey and Arslan Yabgu or in the 11th-12th centuries when Anatolia was conquered by Seljukians.

The pressure of foreign tribes or the struggle of dominance among themselves is another reason for the migration. For instance, Kitans' attack in the 11th century brought about Turks' migration to the West. The elimination of the Uighur State in Orkhun-Yenisei by the Kyrgyz, another Turkic tribe, in 840, resulted in the dissolution of Kutlu Yurt Otugen and Uighurs were forced to migrate to the southern regions such as Turfan, Kan su, and the Agricultural Basin. Perhaps the famous "Migration" epic of the Uighurs is the memory of this event. Kutlu Mountain which symbolizes the homeland in the epic, is given to the Chinese and the mountain is torn apart by the Chinese, leading to catastrophe and drought in the country, and all living and non-living creatures groan "immigration, immigration". Uyghurs complying with this divine command come to Beşbalıg and establish five different cities. This sacred homeland understanding, which is not seen in primitive nomads, is riveted by independence.

Turks chose to emigrate rather than lose their independence and searched for new homeland for themselves. This strong tradition of creating homeland in Turks and establishing a state are another important reason that drives our ancestors to new conquests. In time, this conquest understanding, which aims to bring peace and tranquility to the world, and to rule people with justice and equality, has led to the emergence of the "Ideal of Global Dominance" in the Turks. Therefore, Turkish migrations are different from the primitive nomadism.

Nomads are primitive societies that do not recognize the concept of homeland and that do not know where to stop. The Turks, in the country which they accept as home land, are a "ritualized" nation who lives between certain summer pastures and winter quarters. The Turks have set up cities since the day they entered the stage of history.

CHAPTER-NINE

ATATURK, THE GREATEST TURKISH NATIONALIST

EVERY TURKISH IDEALIST <u>MUST KNOW THAT</u> <u>ATATÜRK IS THE GREATEST TURKIST</u>

The last great grandson of Oğuz Kagan, Mustafa Kemal Atatürk, is undoubtedly the most important Turkish nationalist of all times. He has not only been a symbol for his own race, but also a symbol of independence war of people who live in many foreign captivities. Of course a book will not be enough to tell him. However, everyone from the right to the far left, from the separatists to those who still seek remedy in American mandate or in the European Union, all groups use him in accordance with their interests. The Turkish nationalists, who are the only true followers of Mustafa Kemal's ideas and actions, continue to pursue his ideals without making propaganda.

This Turkish nationalist, who had a great political intelligence, took very smart steps as long as he was the head of the state. He acted in the threats against the Turkish state and nation without fearing anything and without making concessions. This great man, during the rebuilding of the state, took care of everything by himself. The preparation of the constitution, the establishment of the reforms, the substitution of the institutions of language and history, the opening of the Faculty of Languages and History-Geography are the most obvious indicators of this. In fact, the issue of the proclamation of the Republican regime is a wonder on its own.

It is probably the basic point of Atatürk's success to do everything according to the conditions of science and age. He created from a multi-national structure, a nation state. While saying "peace at home peace in the world" he never gave up on the interests of the Turkish State. Mustafa Kemal was a good, honest, forward-looking state figure, and a large part of the Turkish society supported him. That those who came after him could not succeed in realising his ideals was perhaps not his fault but lack of sight and stolidity of those who inherited Atatürk's fortune by some means or other. The lifetime of this magnificent person who associates this creation superiority to being Turk was unfortunately not enough to realize what he would do. This is a misfortune of the Republic of Turkey.

Mustafa Kemal, who made definite decisions that could be taken quickly in the face of the events, never thought to procrastinate these as present day politicians do. In other words, he never put off for tomorrow what he could do today, as the saying goes.

Mustafa Kemal was a complete Turkish nationalist. Nowadays, although this feature of his is intentionally aimed by the agenda of Ataturk's enemies who are seemingly Kemalist, even though he is given various titles **he was 100 percent Turkish and Turkist. The past of those who try to deny this should be thoroughly investigated.**

What Mustafa Kemal did and said is obvious. Fortunately, all these documents are available. Otherwise, certain people would put him into various moulds which reflect no characteristics of his and they actually do this as we mentioned above.

Today, Ataturk's Turkism and other important aspects are ignored. Isn't the person who says "how happy is the one who says i'm a Turk" the greatest Turkish nationalist?

Why do we never hear of this or similar narratives of Atatürk from those who are disgusted by the name

Ataturk, who deliberately express their level of love and loyalty to Turkishness and to Atatürk by calling him Mustafa Kemal? If God lets me, I will take back Mosul, Kirkuk and the Islands. I will add Western Thrace including Thessaloniki into the borders of Turkey! These words are dedicated to those who deflect Atatürk's words "Peace at Home, Peace in the World".

Atatürk also proudly stated the following;

An Istanbul newspaper will also be understood by a Turk in Kashgar.
- On the face of the world, there is no nation that is greater than, older than, and purer than the Turkish nation and there never been in the history of mankind.

- Every place where Turkish people live is in the national borders,

- My only superiority in life is to be born Turkish,

-We are directly national and Turkish nationalist,

- The foundation of our republic is the Turkish community,The more the members of this community are full of Turkish culture, the stronger the republic based on that community,

-Do not interpret me as an extraordinary person. My sole extraordinariness is that I was born as a Turk.

-This is Turkish: Lightning, hurricane, the sun that illuminates the world,

- If you find some extraordinariness in me, associate it with my being Turkish.

-This country was Turkish in history and today it is Turkish and it will live forever as Turkish,

Whatever the premises of education are, our children and youth must be taught, before everything, the necessity to fight against all the elements that are enemy to Turkey's future, to their own personalities and to national conventions.

-The more Turkish child gets to know his ancestors, the more power he will find in himself to make great things.

One of the most prominent characteristics of nationality is language. The people who consider themselves Turkish nation must speak Turkish first and foremost. If a person who does not speak Turkish and claims that he is loyal to Turkish culture and to his community, believing in this will not be accurate. Let us work not for ourselves but for the nation we belong to. This is the biggest of the works,

The Turkish Nation has a high character, the Turkish Nation is industrious, the Turkish Nation is intelli gent,

A Turk is noble only for he is a Turk. Most of us do not remember the father of our grandfather. We find all our pride in being Turkish,

From Atatürk's Tenth Year Speech

We have done a lot of work in less time. The greatest of these works, whose foundation is Turkish heroism and noble Turkish culture, is the Republic of Turkey,
The character of the Turkish nation is high. The Turkish nation is industrious, the Turkish nation is intelligent. Because the Turkish nation has learned to overcome the difficulties in national unity and togetherness. And because the torch the Turkish nation holds in its hands and minds on the path of civilization and advancement that the Turkish nation is walking, is positive science,

G. Atatürk

Turkic Languages

Turkic Languages:
Karluk Languages:
    Yellow Uyghur
    Salar
    Uyghur
    Uzbek
Kipchak Languages:
    Balkar
    Bashkir
    Crimean Tatar
    Karaim
    Karakalpak
    Karachay
    Kazakh
    Kirgiz
    Kumyk
    Noghay
    Tatar
    (Baraba Tatar)
North-Eastern Turkic:
    Dolgan
Yakut

North Turkic:
    Altay
    Khakassian
    Karagassian
    [Tofalarisch]
    Shor
Oghuz Turkic:
    Afshar
    Azeri Turkic
    Gagauz
    Turkic
    Kashgay
    Trukhmen
    Turkmen
Other Turkic Languages:
    Khalaj
    Khorasan Turkic
    Chuvash
    (Dialects   in parentheses)
    [Name variants in square brackets]

ALTAIC LANGUAGES

URALIC LANGUAGES

AMo Mongolic languages

AMo1	Mongolian / Ordos
AMo2	Oirat / Kalmyk
AMo3	Buryat
AMo4	Dagur
AMo5	Monguor-Santa
AMo6	Shira Yugur
AMo7	Moghol

AK Korean

AJ Japonic languages

agglutinating languages,
so the language family
is in dispute

ATu Tungusic languages

ATu1	Northern Tungusic (Tungus)
ATu2	Southeastern Tungusic (Amur)
ATu3	Southwestern Tungusic (Manchu)

AT Turkic languages

AT1	Qashqai	AT13	Chuvash
AT2	Salar	AT14	Karaim
AT3	Yugur	AT15	Turkmen
AT4	Khalaj	AT16	Azerbaijani
AT5	Khakas	AT17	Tatar
AT6	Tuvan	AT18	Crimean Tatar
AT7	Shor	AT19	Bashkir
AT8	Altay	AT20	Uzbek
AT9	Tofa	AT21	Kyrgyz
AT10	Karakalpak	AT22	Gagauz
AT11	Kazakh	AT23	Afshar
AT12	Turkish	AT24	Khorasani Turkic

AT25	Uyghur
AT26	Nogai
AT27	Karachay-Balkar
AT28	Kumyk
AT29	Trukhmen
AT30	Dolgan
AT31	Sakha

From a geographical point of view the
Turkic languages AT26 - AT29 are also
belonging to the group of the otherwise
isolated Caucasian languages.

UF Finno-Ugric

UF1	Baltic Finnic
UF2	Sami languages
UF3	Permic languages
UF4	Volga-Finnic
UF5	Hungarian
UF6	Ob-Ugric

US Samoyedic

US1	Northern group
US2	Southern group

UY Yukaghir

The affiliation to the Uralic
languages is in dispute

Sketch: Dr. phil. İhsan Yilmaz Bayraktarli
Cartography: Dipl.-Geogr. Maximilian Dörrbecker

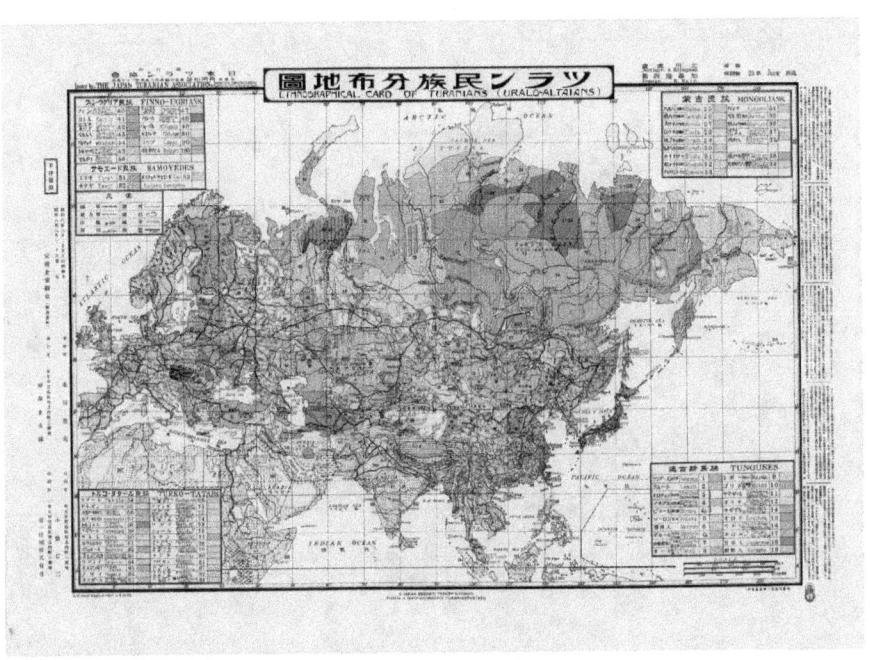

A provocative and very rare ethnographic map of Eurasia promoting the concept of Pan-Turanism, which asserted ancestral connections between the Hungarian and Japanese peoples

.

Number of Native Speakers in the Turkic Language Family

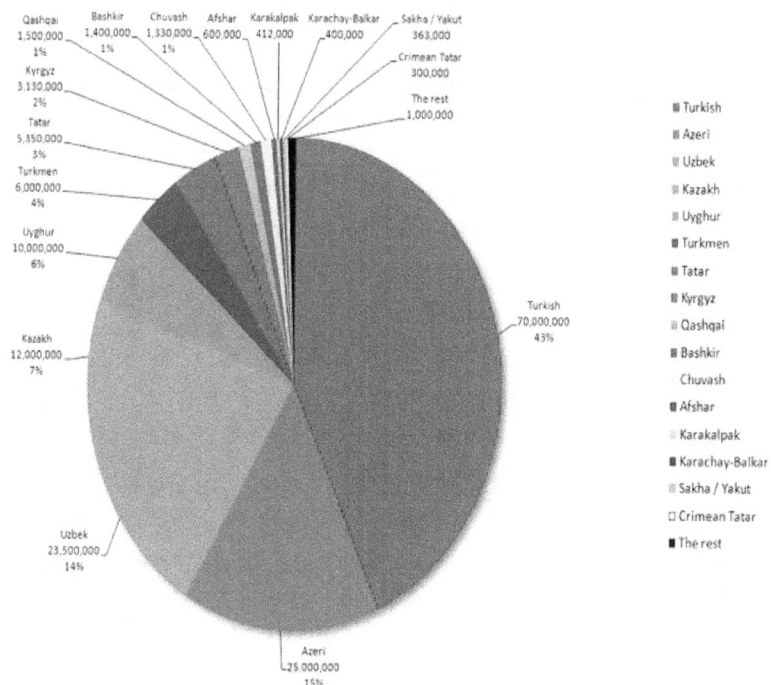

Qashqai 1,500,000 1%
Bashkir 1,400,000 1%
Chuvash 1,330,000 1%
Afshar 600,000
Karakalpak 412,000
Karachay-Balkar 400,000
Sakha / Yakut 363,000
Kyrgyz 3,130,000 2%
Tatar 5,350,000 3%
Turkmen 6,000,000 4%
Uyghur 10,000,000 6%
Kazakh 12,000,000 7%
Uzbek 23,500,000 14%
Crimean Tatar 300,000
The rest 1,000,000
Turkish 70,000,000 43%
Azeri 25,000,000 15%

- ■ Turkish
- ■ Azeri
- ▨ Uzbek
- ▨ Kazakh
- ▨ Uyghur
- ■ Turkmen
- ■ Tatar
- ■ Kyrgyz
- ▨ Qashqai
- ■ Bashkir
-   Chuvash
- ■ Afshar
- ▨ Karakalpak
- ■ Karachay-Balkar
- ▨ Sakha / Yakut
- ▢ Crimean Tatar
- ■ The rest